Let's Team Up!

A Checklist for Teachers, Paraeducators and Principals

by Kent Gerlach, Ed.D.

DUDE PUBLISHING
A Division of
National Professional Resources, Inc.
www.NPRinc.com

Let's Team Up! A Checklist for Teachers, Paraeducators and Principals
Cover/Book Design & Production by Andrea Cerone,
National Professional Resources, Inc., Port Chester, NY

© 2015 Kent Gerlach, Ed.D.

Dude Publishing
A Division of National Professional Resources, Inc.
Toll free: (800) 453-7461
Phone: (914) 937-8879

Visit our web site: www.NPRinc.com

Printed in the United States of America

ISBN 978-1-935609-94-0

Acknowledgments

"Let's Team Up!" is intended to respond to the changes in school policies and practices that have led to today's focus on improved teamwork and communications in team settings. It responds to the mandates of the Elementary and Secondary Education Act (ESEA) and Individuals with Disabilities Education Act (IDEA) which call for defined roles of paraeducators and those who supervise them. *"Let's Team Up!"* also responds to the critical need for teachers, paraeducators and principals to fully understand their roles in the team process. Role clarification is extremely important for team success. Teachers, paraeducators and principals need to understand their individual responsibilities.

This book uses a checklist format which makes it easier for all members of the team to work together more effectively and to understand their roles in the instructional process.

I would like to thank the staff at National Professional Resources, Inc. who made this book possible—most importantly Robert (Bob) Hanson, who encouraged me to publish "Let's Team Up!" Also, Joseph Casbarro who gave me guidance throughout. I would also like to thank Helene Hanson and Andrea Cerone who assisted me in the publication process.

And to my numerous colleagues, paraeducators, teachers and principals who contributed by offering specific suggestions, I offer a special thanks. I have appreciated their dedication to the issues effecting paraeducators and those who supervise them.

This checklist is a synthesis of several resources and websites that are listed in the resource section in the back of the book. When we all "team up" and work together, everyone becomes successful.

About the Author

Kent Gerlach, Ed.D. has been recognized nationally for his contributions, research and publications on paraeducator issues. Research topics have included paraeducator employment, training, supervision, evaluation, and legal and ethical issues.

Kent has presented numerous professional development workshops for teachers, paraeducators and administrators throughout the United States and Canada. In addition, he has served as a Keynote presenter at numerous educational conferences and meetings.

Kent has co-edited several articles, book chapters, and professional development materials dealing with the roles of paraeducators and their supervisors. These include effective communication and team building strategies, and the legal and ethical issues concerning paraeducator roles in instruction. He co-authored the texts *Supervising Paraeducators in Educational Settings and Paraeducators in the Schools,* both published by Pro-ed, Austin, Texas.

"Let's Team Up! A Checklist for Teachers, Paraeducators and Principals" is published by Dude Publishing, a division of National Professional Resources, Inc. (NPR, Inc.).

Currently Kent is a Professor in the School of Education and Kinesiology at Pacific Lutheran University (PLU) in Tacoma, Washington. He has held faculty appointments at the University of Washington (Seattle), University of Texas (Austin), University of Hawaii and Augustana College (Sioux Falls).

He is the recipient of several teaching awards including the PLU Faculty Achievement Award and the PLU Teaching Excellence Award. Kent currently serves as a consultant to the Washington State Office of the Superintendent of Public Instruction and the Washington State Professional Educators Standards Board.

He is also an educational consultant with Pacific Training Associates in Seattle, Washington and has served as consultant to several national organizations including the Council for Exceptional Children (CEC), the National Education Association (NEA), American Speech and Hearing Association (ASHA), the IDEA Partnerships, the U.S. Department of Education (OSEP), Recruiting Teachers, Inc., Boston, MA, and the National Directors of Special Education (NASDE).

Currently he serves on the Editorial Boards of the Council for Exceptional Children (Division of Autism and Developmental Disabilities (DADD) and the Teacher Education Division (TED) and the Thompson Publishing Group, Title One Monitor.

Kent continues to be a recognized and respected advocate for educational policy and standards concerning paraeducators and their supervision.

Contents

Discussing Curriculum and Instruction
Working with Parents and Families
Discussing Student Behavior
Discussing Data Collection and Student Observation
Discussing Student Monitoring
Promoting Training and Professional Development
Giving Feedback

What Are Your Major Responsibilities?
Learning School Policies and Procedures
Questions to Ask the First Week on the Job
Working with Teachers and Other Supervisors
Performing Assigned Tasks
Supporting Curriculum and Instruction
Dealing with Student Behavior
Assisting Students with Special Needs
What You Need to Know About a Student's
    Individualized Education Program
Obtaining Training and Professional Development
Maintaining Ethical Conduct and Professionalism

What Are Your Major Responsibilities?
An Effective Team Leader
Recruiting and Hiring Paraeducators
Good Job Descriptions are Important
Basic Elements of a Good Job Description
Creating a Professional Climate
Providing Building and Job Orientation

Sharing School Policies and Procedures

Supporting the Teacher-Paraeducator Team

Providing Training and Professional Development

Evaluation of Paraeducator Training

Evaluating Paraeducators and the Teachers
Who Supervise Them

End of the Year Program Evaluation

Sample Evaluation Checklist

Guiding Principles for Paraeducator Employment, Roles,
Preparation and Supervision

District and/or Building Assessment of Paraeducator Issues

Print and Video

Web Sites

Glossary of Terms

Abbreviations/Acronyms

What Motivates Members of the Team

Introduction

The changing landscape of public education has had a significant impact on the roles of the personnel who serve in our schools. Personnel shortages, increasing numbers of English language learners, and the rising enrollment of students with disabilities and other special needs are just some of the factors that make the need for a dynamic school team more important than ever before. In this challenging environment, paraeducators play an increasingly critical role in improving student achievement.

Paraeducators—also known as paraprofessionals, instructional assistants, educational assistants, teacher assistants and teacher aides—are school employees who work under the direction of certified or licensed staff members to help provide instructional and other services to students and their families. "Para" means "along side of," and like their counterparts in the legal and medical fields—paralegals and paramedics—paraeducators assist and support the educational team in a variety of ways. The term "paraeducator" can be defined as a school employee who assists and supports teacher-directed instruction (Gerlach, 2003). In most districts, paraeducators live in the school community. They sometimes speak the language of the students, and provide a special liaison to the community and its culture. Many paraeducators entered the field by first serving as a parent volunteer.

In the last 40 years, the number of paraeducators in the United States has increased dramatically. One reason for this increase is that more and more children need small-group and individual help. Under federal legislation such as the Elementary and Secondary Education Act (ESEA) and the

Individuals with Disabilities Education Act (IDEA), paraeducators may assist with instruction. In most school districts, the role of the paraeducator has evolved from clerical assistant to instructional assistant.

Until recently, however, staff development and training on the appropriate role of paraeducators has been very limited—not only for paraeducators, but also for teachers and principals. This is changing, in part because of recent federal and state legislation. These acts require appropriate training and supervision of paraeducators, and target the need to establish policy and guidelines for paraeducator supervision, responsibilities, role clarification, preparation and career development.

How Can This Checklist Help You?

Let's Team Up! provides helpful tips for teachers on working effectively with paraeducators; practical suggestions for paraeducators on clarifying their duties and relationships with students, teachers and administrative staff; and advice for principals on supervision, training and evaluation.

The goal is to promote recognition and respect among the members of the educational team. Effective communication is the most important factor for any team, and the information in this book will help team members better communicate as they work together for the benefit of students and families.

When every member of the school team is successful, the entire school community wins.

What Is the Focus of This Checklist?

The focus of this checklist is to clarify and strengthen the roles and responsibilities of teachers, paraeducators and principals as they relate to each other.

Who Can Benefit from This Checklist?

▶ Teachers
▶ Paraeducators
▶ Principals
▶ Other administrators, such as directors of special education, Title I, and bilingual programs
▶ Teacher educators
▶ Student/preservice teachers
▶ Speech therapists
▶ Physical therapists
▶ Occupational therapists
▶ School nurses
▶ Parents and families
▶ School board members
▶ Staff developers and inservice coordinators
▶ Human resources personnel
▶ Early childhood providers
▶ Community and technical college staff
▶ Teacher training program providers
▶ Policymakers
▶ State Education Department personnel

When Should This Checklist Be Used?

This checklist (which is actually a series of checklists) should be used for paraeducator and teacher orientation, as well as throughout the year whenever paraeducators are part of an instructional team. It is especially beneficial to team members as they begin their work together. Teachers and paraeducators can use it to formulate questions and clarify their roles. Principals can us it to strengthen their roles as instructional and building leaders. Numerous school districts have also used it with new staff as an orientation handbook.

How Should This Checklist Be Used?

This checklist can be used as a guide or handbook by individual team members or as an instructional guide in team meetings, staff development workshops and preservice training. It can serve as a valuable tool for helping everyone gain a clear understanding of their roles and responsibilities as members of the instructional team.

This book consists of five main sections:

Building a Winning Team informs teachers, paraeducators and principals about why they should "team up," outlines the 10 characteristics of an effective team and explains how to orient a new team member. It also gives strategies for promoting and assessing team effectiveness.

The Teacher's Role helps teachers and other certified or licensed personnel to: orient paraeducators to the school and classroom; develop appropriate ways to supervise, manage and direct the work of paraeducators; assign tasks and give directions; discuss curriculum and student behavior; provide on-the-job training; and give useful feedback to paraeducators.

The Paraeducator's Role helps paraeducators ask the right questions about school policies and procedures. It provides a framework for: communicating and working with their supervisors; performing assigned tasks; assisting and supporting curriculum and instruction; dealing with student behavior; assisting students with special needs; training and professional development; and ethics and professionalism.

The Principal's Role helps principals and other school administrators: interview and hire qualified candidates for paraeducator positions; create a professional and supportive climate; provide building and job orientation; share school policies and procedures; support teacher-paraeducator teams; and provide and design appropriate training and professional development.

The Resources Section contains a list of organizations and multimedia resources (books and web sites) on related topics. There is also a comprehensive **Glossary of Terms** that provides helpful definitions related to a variety of educational topics, followed by a listing of **Abbreviations/Acronyms**.

We encourage all readers—whether teachers, paraeducators or administrators—to review *Let's Team Up!* in its entirety. It will give you a better understanding of your colleagues' roles, responsibilities and professional duties, which in turn will help you to better perform your job.

We also encourage readers to be flexible in using the components of the checklist. Situations, roles and responsibilities may be different in each local school district. These lists are intended as a guide to help build team effectiveness and clarify the roles and responsibilities of each team member. In using the checklist, the reader will find that the responsibilities of paraeducators, teachers and administrators overlap to some extent. However, there are certain roles that the teacher and administrator must maintain for ethical and legal reasons. Role clarification is a "must" for effective teamwork.

"The job of a paraeducator is a test. It is only a test. If it had been an actual job, you would have been given instructions on where to go and what to do."

—Kent Gerlach

"More than ever before, children need to see adults working well together. This comes from respecting and recognizing each other."

—Kent Gerlach

The Story of Sara "The Para"

Sara had been serving as a parent volunteer in her son's second grade classroom. One day she saw an ad on the school bulletin board for an opening for a classified position—The Title: Paraeducator. The job announcement  gave her little information about the duties required of a paraeducator. In fact, all it said was "duties as assigned." Sara had a lot of questions about the job. She wanted to know "what are paraeducators?" "and what do they do?" She needed a job and she knew she wanted this job. The hours were good and she knew she wanted to work with children. She had thought about going back to college, but she did not want all the responsibilities of a teacher.

So Sara went to seek the advise of the wisest, most highly respected counselor in the land.

"Wise counselor," Sara began, "it has always been my dream to work with children. I want to stimulate the minds of the young people of our land. I want to lead them down the road of knowledge. I want to be a great role model for children. Please tell me the secret of becoming a paraeducator."

"Your goal is a commendable one, Sara. However, you must understand that not everyone will succeed as a paraeducator. First you must overcome several major obstacles," said the wise counselor.

"I am ready to meet the challenge," Sara answered bravely. "This is a most unusual career choice," said the knowing counselor. Sara looked concerned. "What skills do I need for this job?", asked Sara. "Well, let's put it this way," said the knowing counselor, "a para's job is special—you'll learn as you go. There are few pre-skills or training required." "Do I have to take any tests?" asked Sara.

"Sara," said the learned counselor, "a para's job is a test. Just remember PARA'S ARE SPECIAL!" "Do I need a certificate, a permit, or a credential?" "Oh no," said the counselor. "In some states you might, but in most states you don't. Keep in mind, Sara, there are very few guidelines or standards for this position. Just remember, Sara, PARA'S ARE SPECIAL."

Tell me more. I really want this job."

"Well," said the wise counselor, "school districts frequently hire paraeducators who have been a successful parent volunteer. You have done that! You are already part of the community. You will be a great para, Sara."

"I'm very excited", said Sara, "what else should I do?" "Just fill out the district application form," said the counselor. "Will I have to wait long before I know if I will be hired?" "Oh no, in most cases, Sara, para's will begin the job the day after they are hired." "The next day?" Sara questioned.

"What about an orientation to the job? Is there time to observe the teachers or children?" "No Sara. There is no orientation to this job. Remember, PARA'S ARE SPECIAL!" "What about a handbook? What about district policies?"

"If you are lucky you will receive written guidelines or poli-cies. You might even receive a handbook, but remember most districts don't have written guidelines or a handbook or written policies! Sara, you will do fine, Trust me! Remember, Sara, PARA'S ARE SPECIAL!!"

"Many para's start by working on the playground, or in the lunchroom. They might give you a whistle. They will wish you good luck, and then you will be on your own."

"When do I meet my supervisors?" Sara asked. "You will meet them tomorrow." "What children will I be assigned to?" Sara asked. "You will be assigned to the most difficult children—the ones with learning and behavior problems. The ones who need the most attention." "How will I know what to do?" said Sara. "Well," said the wise counselor, "a lot of it will come naturally."

"Remember," said the wise counselor, "Asking for assistance is a strength not a weakness. Ask questions, ask for assistance." "But who will I ask?" said Sara. "You will be assigned to one supervising teacher and in some cases you may be supervised by several teachers." "Will they all tell me the same thing?" asked Sara.

The wise counselor responded by saying, "Because most teachers are not trained to supervise paras, each teacher could see your job differently. But, I am sure they will give you guidance. It will be ok, trust me."

So Sara completed the application, and the principal hired her. And as the wise counselor said, she began her work the very next day, with no orientation.

The principal told Sara that she would be working with three different supervisors in three different programs and also be a playground assistant and lunchroom guard. "Will I get any breaks during the day?" "Para's don't need breaks," said the principal.

The principal then informed her of the schedule. "Each morning, after escorting the students off the bus, and monitoring the bathrooms, you will assist in the Title One program." Sara asked, "What is a Title One program?" "Oh, it will be explained to you tomorrow, your first day," said the principal.

"During third period, you will be working with a boy with autism." "But I'm not sure what autism is," said Sara. "Oh, it will be explained to you tomorrow by the supervising teacher. In the meantime you might wish to check out a book on autism from the library. In the afternoon you will be assigned to two children who are part of the ESL Program. These children just moved here from Russia and do not speak any English." "But I don't know Russian," said Sara. "Don't worry ," said the principal , "it will come naturally. In the meantime I suggest you read up on the Russian language tonight."

"When do I start work?" asked Sara. "ASAP, How about tomorrow," said the principal. The principal responded by saying, "Your day starts when the first bell rings. Your day will end when the bell sounds at the end of the day. In other words, when the children leave." "But that doesn't leave any time to meet with my supervisor," said Sara.

"We know that can be a problem," said the principal. Paras must use their time well. Paras must be flexible. You'll find a time. You'll see each other in the halls. Don't worry it will work. We've done it this way for years. It will come naturally."

That night Sara listened to Russian language tapes, and she read several books on autism. She still had no idea what a

Title One program was. But Sara knew she would find out tomorrow.

The next day arrived, the first day on the job. Nervously Sara met her first supervisor. This teacher just got her teaching degree a few months earlier.

The teacher asked, "Sara, what is a para, what does a para do?"

"I thought you would tell me that," said Sara.

The teacher said, "How would I know what you do? I never had training on that. I guess we will have to learn together, it will be ok. It will come naturally. Together we will learn. Together we will succeed after all, PARA'S ARE SPECIAL!!"

So what is the moral of this story? Blessed are the flexible for they shall not be broken!

Author's Comments: Too many paraeducators have identified with "Sara." I used humor in this story to make a point. By using the checklist in *Lets Team Up!,* all team members will have a better understanding of their roles and responsibilities. Teachers, paraeducators and principals will be more effective team members, benefiting students and families.

Chapter 1:
Building A Winning Team

Pine Bluff School in the Southwest has won numerous awards for staff development and school achievement. This Title I school serves many students with special needs in inclusion classrooms. In addition, nearly 50% of the students speak English as a second language. Five years ago, Pine Bluff was struggling to adjust to these challenges. Today, it's an award-winning school. What turned Pine Bluff around?

The principal, with the support of a dedicated staff, instituted a three-year plan with the goal of improving communication, collaboration and teamwork throughout the school. Both teachers and paraeducators receive training on their roles, and the school district has an extensive paraeducator staff development program in collaboration with the local community college. Paraeducators are also included in staff meetings, and the school provides a set planning time for teachers and paraeducators to communicate. In addition, the school provides a peer mentoring program for beginning teachers and paraeducators.

What can other schools learn from the Pine Bluff experience? What are some of the factors that contribute to building a dynamic school team?

BUILDING A WINNING TEAM

The interdependent working relationship of today's teachers, paraeducators and principals is often like a jigsaw puzzle. Unfortunately, the players don't have a picture on the front of a box to know what the puzzle is supposed to look like when it's finished. Sometimes they don't even have all the pieces.

That's why, in today's education climate, the most successful schools operate as a team. School personnel understand the importance of a good working relationship and are focused on team goals. They form relationships that are built on effective communication, trust, respect and recognition. When teachers, paraeducators and principals team up to connect the pieces of the puzzle, students are the ultimate beneficiaries.

The Team Building Process

Step 1: Establish team composition.

Step 2: Define the purpose and goals of the team.

Step 3: Clarify roles and responsibilities.

Step 4: Establish team rules (norms and policies).

Step 5: Integrate individual personalities and strengths.

Step 6: Manage team performance (leadership and
          supervision).

Step 7: Evaluate team effectiveness.

Characteristics of a New Paraeducator and Teacher Team

According to a review of research on team effectiveness done by Abelson and Woodman (1983), a team that has just formed usually has some or all of the following characteristics:

1. There is considerable confusion as to roles that team members must assume.

2. There is confusion as to the social and professional relationships among members of the team.

3. Individuals have some assets or competencies relative to the team's purpose. However, some people may be unaware of how their skills or knowledge relate to team goals. Perhaps more importantly, some individuals may be unaware of (or may not value) the strengths and competencies of others, or may not appreciate their relationship to team goals.

4. While there may be some understanding of short-range goals (e.g., why the team was brought together), understanding of long-range goals is likely to be more elusive.

5. In the absence of established norms, rules or policy, there is considerable confusion about how the team will operate, how decisions will be made, and so on.

6. Team members (and particularly leaders) do not pay much early attention to social and professional relationships, being more likely to focus initially on the task.

These characteristics are important for us to consider when focusing on the teacher-paraeducator team.

If a team is to be effective, the team must agree on the team's purpose. Members must see the benefits of working together. The mission and goals of the team must be developed with input from all team members. Roles and responsibilities of both the teacher and paraeducator must be clearly defined. Clear expectations are given by the supervising teacher in order to get the job done. Information is shared in a timely manner, and the time the team meets together is effective and productive.

Teaming depends on effective communication. Effective communication expresses a team member's beliefs, ideas, needs or feelings. For effective team performance, "communication" must facilitate the free flow or exchange of ideas, information and instruction that contribute to common understanding.

When ideas are shared, there is opportunity for evaluation and input that can build even better ideas. From each new experience, more ideas can be developed and tried. Successful communication results in a mutual understanding of what was said and what was heard.

The following questions can be used to assess teacher/paraeducator team effectiveness:

- Do all team members understand team goals?
- Are all team members committed to these goals?
- Are team members concerned and interested in each other?
- Do team members have the emotional maturity to acknowledge and confront conflict openly?

- Do team members listen to others with openness and understanding?
- Do all team members value one another's contributions?
- Do team members feel comfortable contributing ideas and solutions to problems?
- Do team members encourage and appreciate comments about team efforts?
- Are team meetings held at a specific time?
- Is leadership effective?
- Is constructive feedback given freely to improve decision-making?
- Is information shared willingly?
- Are team members willing to communicate their concerns?

Remember, it is essential to identify all the pieces of the puzzle so that students can benefit from the entire team.

Why Team Up?

- Team members support and mentor each other.

- Teams reduce the feeling of isolation that is common in education.

- Teams foster professional and personal growth by members sharing knowledge and skills with each other.

- Teams develop unique, creative and flexible solutions to problems.

- Teams maximize each member's potential, strengths and contributions.

- Teams establish goals together, and team members feel a sense of ownership toward these goals.

- A team spirit develops when people work well together.

"A successful team effort is not a mysterious or magical event that just 'happens' because fate brought the right group together. Real team-work happens as a result of a deliberate and well thought out plan, executed by a skilled team leader who has a clear vision, specific goals, and a definite strategy to get people to work well together."

—Robert Zenger

Ten Characteristics of an Effective Team

1. All team members understand why the team exists and are committed to accomplishing the mission and goals of the team.

2. Team members know what needs to be done, and by whom, to achieve team goals.

3. Team members know their roles in getting tasks done and how to use the skills and expertise of each member most effectively.

4. Decision-making leadership and supervision guidelines are clearly understood by all team members.

5. Team members feel their unique personalities and strengths are appreciated and well utilized.

6. Team members are able to share ideas and give input into discussions.

7. Team members find team meetings efficient and productive. Teams meet on a regular schedule.

8. Team members know clearly when the team has been successful and share in the success equally.

9. Staff development is provided and is taken advantage of by team members.

10. Feedback is provided to all team members.

— Adapted from various business journals

Orienting a New Team Member

When a new teacher, paraeducator or administrator joins the team, does it make you a little nervous or apprehensive? It often signals brand new expectations and a new set of rules. Here are several suggestions for making a positive adjustment to a new team member.

☐ Do everything you can to create a good first impression. The first impression is often a lasting one.

☐ Be flexible and open to change. Don't dwell on the way things were done in the past. New conditions may call for new procedures.

☐ Help your new team member as much as you can. Remember that the new person has to adjust to a new situation, too. Stress mentorship.

☐ Find out which objectives and priorities are most important to your new team member.

☐ As problems and questions come up, address them immediately. Deal with them openly and honestly rather than going behind the backs of team members.

☐ Be prepared for change. Some things are beyond your control. If you expect things to work out well, they probably will.

☐ Patience, understanding, initiative and hard work will go a long way toward resolving most issues.

Promoting the Team

☐ Commit yourself to being part of the team.

☐ Emphasize cooperation, not competition.

☐ Focus on team and student outcomes.

☐ Accentuate and build on team strengths.

☐ Approach time from a team standpoint, remembering that different people perceive time differently. Develop an ongoing dialogue on how best to use team time.

☐ Take time to communicate effectively. This involves being a good listener as well as a good speaker.

☐ When instructing others, be sure to provide complete information and clear instructions. Check to be sure your teammates fully understand everything that was asked of them.

☐ Improve team methods of planning and coordinating projects and activities.

☐ Give team members plenty of advance notice for team meetings, deadlines, etc.

☐ Make sure team members are well informed of any programmatic changes.

☐ Set aside regular time slots for meeting with team members.

☐ Ask team members for ideas on how to improve team relationships and roles.

☐ Look for ways to save time for the people you work with.

☐ Follow a written agenda to make sure your team meetings are productive.

☐ Show up for meetings and turn in assignments on time.

Assessing the Team

Have team members check whether the following statements are true for their team.

- [ ] Team members understand team goals.
- [ ] Team members are committed to these goals.
- [ ] Team members are supportive of each other's roles and responsibilities.
- [ ] Team members have the emotional maturity to acknowledge and confront conflict openly.
- [ ] Team members listen to others with openness and understanding.
- [ ] Team members feel comfortable contributing ideas and solutions to problems.
- [ ] Team members recognize, reward and give feedback on team performance.
- [ ] Team members encourage and appreciate comments about team efforts.
- [ ] Team meetings are held at a specific time and on a regular basis.
- [ ] Constructive feedback is given freely to improve decision making.
- [ ] Information is shared freely. Input is solicited from all team members.
- [ ] Concerns are communicated openly.
- [ ] The spirit of cooperation is stronger than the spirit of competition.
- [ ] Team meetings end with a sense of accomplishment and on a positive note.

Team Assessment Review

The form below is an example of how to assess the function-ality of a team based on the previous page.

Yes	No	
		Do all team members understand team goals?
		Are all team members committed to these goals?
		Do team members acknowledge and confront conflict openly?
		Do team members listen to others with open-ness and understanding?
		Do all team members value one another's contributions?
		Do team members feel comfortable contributing ideas and solutions to problems?
		Do team members show appreciation to one another and recognize and celebrate team performance?
		Do team members encourage and appreciate comments about team efforts?
		Are team meetings held at a place where all have equal eye contact?
		Are team meetings held at a specific time?
		Are team meetings held at a location free from interruption?
		Is the spirit of cooperation stronger than the spirit of competition among team members?

Yes	No	
		Is leadership effective?
		Does everyone feel free to level and be candid with everyone else?
		Do team members "check things out" with supervisor before making decisions?
		Is constructive feedback given freely to improve decision-making?
		Is information shared willingly?
		Are team members willing to communicate their concerns?
		Do team meetings end with a sense of accomplishment and/or on a positive note?

As leaders we can create a positive team atmosphere in which the paraeducator feels their needs are being met.

By sharing ideas and information

By providing training and development

By being available when needed

By providing resources, assistance and support

By demonstrating and observing

By seeking feedback input and ideas

By listening

By working to solve problems together

—Adapted from unknown source

Team Building

☐ Help each other be right, not wrong.

☐ Look for ways to make new ideas work, not for reasons they won't work.

☐ If in doubt, check it out. Don't make negative assumptions about each other.

☐ Help each other be successful and take pride in each other's success.

☐ Speak positively about each other and about your school and educational programs at every opportunity.

☐ Maintain a positive mental attitude no matter what the circumstances are.

☐ Act with initiative and courage, as if it all depends on you.

☐ If you need assistance, ASK! Mentor each other.

☐ Do everything with enthusiasm. It's contagious! Celebrate teamwork!

☐ Enjoy the contributions you make!

Tips for Teams

The following are tips for becoming an effective team member.

☐ Keep the team on task by seeing the vision, goal and task as paramount in all team interactions.

☐ Offer all the relevant knowledge, skills and information you possess to help other team members with their role.

☐ Give colleagues your attention, consideration and respect when they are expressing an idea or making a suggestion.

☐ Contribute to a positive climate by helping people on the team feel comfortable when expressing ideas.

☐ Support one another. Compliment team members for a job well done, show appreciation and celebrate success. Focus on the positive.

☐ Get in the habit of noticing opportunities to praise other team members. Develop a system that helps you remember to notice a praise-worthy effort.

☐ Ask for advice and help when needed. Let your colleagues know you value their opinions. Occasionally ask, "How would you handle this?"

☐ Encourage team members to share their knowledge with you. Let others know how much you value their knowledge and experience.

☐ Prepare to brainstorm. Prior to the team meeting, team members should begin thinking about the agenda, problems or current issues.

☐ Create an action plan. Draw a step-by-step road map of the tasks, timing, staff and resources that you will need.

☐ Listen actively. Learn to listen well. Sort out the team goals and encourage everyone to contribute.

☐ Do not underestimate the value of humor in educational teams.

☐ Be positive. Negativity is like a virus in a team. Use the words that imply positive action and sense of responsibility.

☐ Resolve conflicts through openness. Team conflict is natural and it must be handled in a natural way—through open discussion. When conflicts are suppressed they can have a long-lasting adverse effect on the team interactions.

☐ Encourage open expression of ideas. Create a team atmosphere that at least gives new ideas a fair chance.

☐ Furnish opportunities for personal growth. Team members need to acquire the additional knowledge they need to keep up with change.

☐ Remember that everyone with an idea is important: never forget that when working with others.

☐ Motivate your teammates by creating a positive and energetic mood! Peer influence is a strong force within a team and can lead to positive and innovative results.

☐ Think creatively, explore ideas and empathize with other's thoughts and ideas.

☐ Commit to quality. Ask the question, "How can we improve?" Do this frequently.

☐ Take better control of your time. Keep meetings on track. Make sure there is an agenda.

50 Time Management Tips for Team Success

Maximizing time is a major challenge for each member of a team. Effective use of time takes practice. Review the following time management tips and try applying them as appropriate to your team's needs.

1. Approach time from a team standpoint, remembering that people perceive time differently. Develop an ongoing dialog on how best to use team time.

2. Take time to communicate effectively. This involves being a good listener as well as a good talker. Good communication saves time in the long run and prevents many problems.

3. Improve your own methods of planning and coordinating projects and activities.

4. Be patient with others. Start earlier and allow more lead-time.

5. Discuss objectives, priorities and plans with all team members.

6. Set aside regular time slots for talking with your supervisor and other team members.

7. Analyze everything you do and look for ways to improve. The more ideas you collect, the more likely you are to improve. Seek input from others.

8. Look for ways to save time for the people you work with. Be creative, yet flexible.

9. Make sure your meetings with supervisors and team members are productive. Meet with a clear purpose. Follow an agenda or outline. Think of questions ahead of time.

10. Develop the on-time habit. Show up for meetings and appointments on time, deliver work on time, make sure that others never have to wait for you and encourage others to do the same.

11. Practice the Golden Rule: Treat other people the way you would like to be treated. Show appreciation and help your team by being more generous with your praise than with your criticism.

12. Be a mentor to other team members. Great mentors push your thinking and help you grow in new ways. They alert you to new teaching methods and provide tips for how to handle various situations throughout the year.

13. Take time to write down and clarify your goals and expectations. You might want to focus on one or two projects at a time by setting priorities.

14. Learn to make realistic time estimates.

15. Interrupt others less. Every little thought that pops into your head doesn't have to be communicated immediately to others. Write these thoughts down to discuss later.

16. Pay attention when people talk to you.

17. Compete less and cooperate more. By learning to work with others, you can accomplish far more than you could ever accomplish alone.

18. Slow down a little. Don't be so demanding of yourself and others.

19. Finish what you start before jumping to something else. Leaving a string of unfinished tasks behind you creates problems for everyone on your team.

20. Don't use interruptions as an excuse for letting your mind wander. Train yourself to get right back to the task when the interruption is over.

21. Devote time to seeking the opinions of others and learning from them.

22. Discuss with your supervisor ways to improve communication and accountability.

23. Set aside 10 minutes a day for simple planning. Plan at the same time every day. End each day and meeting with a sense of accomplishment.

24. Once the team has developed a plan, stick to it. Remember that your supervisor is counting on you to follow the plan.

25. Curb your socializing time.

26. Simplify the necessary but mundane chores as much as possible.

27. Organize your workspace. Avoid clutter.

28. Respect others' rights. Learn to be sensitive so you'll avoid becoming offensive.

29. Learn to set goals in your professional and personal life. Prioritize those goals.

30. Stop procrastinating. Break large jobs down into smaller pieces and then focus on one piece at a time. Low priority tasks may be postponed.

31. Learn the positive, that planned change will make your life better. Change doesn't have to be frightening.

32. Use "post-it" notes, a journal or a "white" board to communicate with one another.

33. Try to be a self-starter.

34. Speak up more. Your opinion is valuable. Don't keep your questions to yourself. Asking questions is a strength not a weakness.

35. Pay attention to deadlines. Don't be obsessed with them, but don't forget them either.

36. Learn that perfectionism has its limits. Remember that it's important to do your best, not to be perfect.

37. Realize the value of a positive attitude, humor, integrity.

38. Be sure team goals are realistic.

39. Set time limits on your tasks.

40. Learn to be more tolerant of others. Showing empathy and respect is important.

41. Set goals. What are your long-term goals? Consider all aspects of your life: professional, personal, social, family and community.

42. Establish your priorities. Which of your goals are most important? Separate your goals into those of high value, moderate value and low value.

43. Analyze present time use. Are you using your time to reach your high priority goals? Keep a log or journal for a few days and see.

44. Eliminate time wasters. Spend your time on priority tasks that lead to high priority goals.

45. Recognize the difference between "urgent" and "important." Urgent tasks are those that demand immediate completion; they may or may not lead to your high priority goals.

46. Trust is important for team success. Help one another learn the Do's and Don'ts of school politics and communication.

47. Make a daily list of things to do. Make one list and update it daily; be sure to assign priority to every item on the list.

48. Use written notes to a supervisor to summarize the day (how the lesson or activities went).

49. Use email and text messages.

50. Use the *"Let's Team Up"* checklist to clarify team roles and responsibilities.

Can you think of other time management strategies that will make you and your team more organized and effective?

_____

_____

_____

_____

_____

Chapter 2:
The Teacher's Role

Paula, a special education teacher in a Northwest school district, supervises three paraeducators in an inclusion program. When Paula was interviewed for the position, she wasn't told that she would be supervising three adults—two first-year paraeducators and one veteran paraeducator who was new to the district.

Even though Paula has had very little training on managing and directing the work of paraeducators, she reports that her group is doing well so far, because they have taken a team approach to working together and delivering instruction.

Paula often feels frustrated, however, that so much of the district's paraeducator training falls on teachers. One of her biggest concerns is the lack of communication and planning time. Paula says, "I was taught to plan for students, not other adults in my classroom."

Paula wants to be an effective supervisor, but she's not always sure of the best approach to take. What are Paula's responsibilities and what does she need to know to supervise and direct the work of the paraeducators in her classroom?

ESEA and IDEA call for "appropriate" supervision of paraeducators. What does that mean?

THE TEACHER'S ROLE

Teachers are most often responsible for the direct supervision and management of paraeducators. However, most teachers have had little training or experience supervising another adult in the classroom. Some teachers feel uncomfortable in this important role. It's to everyone's benefit that teachers learn how to effectively direct and manage the work of paraeducators. The teacher gets an instructional assistant who can make a genuine difference in the classroom, the paraeducator gets a meaningful professional experience, the school gets a valuable member of the education team and students benefit from effective teamwork.

Teachers are responsible for planning, scheduling and directing the work of paraeducators. In sum, teachers have become managers of both the education process and the human resources who serve as facilitators of student programs and learning. The following are some suggestions for developing appropriate supervision, direction and management of the paraeducators assigned to you, the teacher.

What Are Your Major Responsibilities?

Teachers are responsible for supervising and integrating paraeducators into learning environments, including:

- ▶ Maintaining effective communication.
- ▶ Clarifying team roles.
- ▶ Planning the tasks that paraeducators will perform.
- ▶ Setting goals for the instructional team.
- ▶ Developing schedules for paraeducators.
- ▶ Appropriately delegating responsibilities to paraeducators and providing feedback.
- ▶ Monitoring the day-to-day performance of paraeducators.
- ▶ Providing an orientation to the classroom.
- ▶ Preparing work assignments for paraprofessionals based on program needs, student objectives, and the skills and experience of the paraeducator.
- ▶ Coaching and mentoring paraeducators.
- ▶ Providing feedback and on-the-job training to paraeducators.
- ▶ Sharing relevant information about paraeducator strengths and training needs with principals or other administrators.
- ▶ Supporting appropriate staff development for paraeducators.
- ▶ Establishing team guidelines.
- ▶ Facilitating problem solving.

To perform these duties, teachers need knowledge of federal and district policies regarding paraeducator employment, roles and responsibilities, placement, evaluation, and training opportunities.

Beginning the School Year

☐ Establish an atmosphere of respect, recognition and open communication.

☐ Meet with paraeducators prior to the first day of school or their first day on the job. Contact the new paraeducator as soon as he/she is hired.

☐ Introduce the paraeducator to other teachers, paraeducators and support professionals in the building.

☐ Discuss school rules and policies regarding student behavior on the playground and in the lunchroom, bathrooms, hallways, library, etc.

☐ Acquaint the paraeducator with school records and the way they are monitored and used.

☐ Show the paraeducator where supplies and materials are kept and how they are obtained.

☐ Discuss building and classroom emergency procedures.

☐ Discuss school safety issues and policies.

☐ Inform parents of the paraeducator's role.

☐ Provide an inventory of supplies and instructional materials and explain the process for ordering additional supplies and instructional material.

"The mediocre teacher tells. The good teacher explains. The superior teacher demonstrates. The great teacher inspires."

—*William Arthur Ward, Author*

Introducing Paraeducators to Your Classroom and Program

☐ Allow the paraeducator to spend a minimum of one day observing your classroom and students, as well as those of other teachers.

☐ Provide an initial orientation to your classroom, including:
- ▶ Daily routines
- ▶ Daily and weekly schedules
- ▶ Instructional procedures
- ▶ Classroom rules and district policy
- ▶ Lesson plan format
- ▶ Procedures for handing in and posting student assignments
- ▶ Handbooks (paraeducator, parent, student, etc.)
- ▶ Substitute handbook
- ▶ Monthly calendar
- ▶ School year calendar
- ▶ Professional dress

☐ Explain the activities that take place at the beginning of each class, such as:
- ▶ Recordkeeping procedures
- ▶ Review the daily schedule
- ▶ Recording attendance
- ▶ Warm-up routines
- ▶ Lunch counts
- ▶ Special services, such as speech therapy and other programs

☐ Explain the activities that take place at the end of each class period or day.

☐ Explain your class policy regarding:
  ▶ Classroom organization
  ▶ Instructional materials
  ▶ Classroom procedures (e.g., posting and handing in assignments, etc.)
  ▶ Room organization and clean-up
  ▶ Instructional technology
  ▶ Dismissing the class and small groups
  ▶ Computer and Internet rules
  ▶ Student rules
  ▶ Bathroom rules
  ▶ Neatness, incomplete work, late or missing work, and make-up work
  ▶ Parent and family communication
  ▶ Classroom safety procedures

☐ Discuss the short- and long-term goals of the class or program and students' strengths, individual weaknesses and goals.

☐ Provide a spot for the paraeducator to put his or her belongings, materials, etc.

☐ Explain jargon and acronyms for which the paraeducator may not have background knowledge. Pages 126-143 of this book (Glossary of Terms & Abbreviations/Acronyms), may be helpful.

Managing Paraeducator Responsibilities

☐ Discuss the state and the district's definition for "para-educator" or other titles used in the district.

☐ Discuss any district policy regarding paraeducator's role in instruction.

☐ Discuss the appropriate instructional roles and responsibilities of the teacher and the paraeducator.

☐ Take time to provide clear instructions and complete information to the paraeducator. Ask yourself the following questions:

▶ Did I explain what task needs to be done and why, how, and where it will be done?

▶ Did I explain how the paraeducator will be observed, evaluated, and supervised?

▶ Did I discuss how the paraeducator will provide feedback to me?

▶ Do I speak a team language, such as "It would be good for both of us if we . . . "?

▶ Did I ask for a specific action, or did I phrase my request in ambiguous terms?

▶ Did I provide a written plan and schedule?

▶ Did I set a mutually agreed-upon deadline when I delegated a task?

▶ Did I confirm important issues in writing?

▶ Did I give the paraeducator appropriate feedback?

▶ Have I determined the training and staff development needs of the paraeducator?

▶ Have I developed a way to document the training I have provided to the paraeducator?

- ☐ Ask about the paraeducator's expectations of you, the instructional supervisor.
- ☐ Share your expectations and work plan for the para-educator.
- ☐ Communicate in a clear and supportive manner.
- ☐ Create and manage schedules.
- ☐ Build a set meeting time, daily or weekly, in your schedule to plan and communicate with the para-educator.
- ☐ Communicate with your principal if there is a problem establishing a set communication time.
- ☐ Discuss how you'll communicate with one another if you don't have a daily meeting time.
- ☐ Provide a clear, daily direction for coordinating plans, schedules, tasks and feedback.
- ☐ Discuss goals, priorities and plans with paraeducators on a daily basis. Do it first thing every morning.
- ☐ Discuss the roles of the substitute and paraeducator when you are absent.
- ☐ Discuss the role of the "parasubstitute" when the para-educator is absent.
- ☐ With input from the paraeducator, develop a para-educator substitute plan or guide.

☐ Make the most of meeting and planning times with the paraeducator by:

  ▶ Communicating the purpose/agenda in advance.
  ▶ Respecting the paraeducator's individuality and utilize his or her talents in classroom activities.
  ▶ Providing instructional leadership and include the paraeducator in planning meaningful assignments with clear directions.
  ▶ Taking a problem-solving approach.
  ▶ Holding the meeting in a site where instructional materials and records are readily available and interruptions are minimized.

☐ Discuss problems and ideas with paraeducators. Ask for their ideas, suggestions and opinions.

☐ Take time to listen to the paraeducator's concerns and questions. Ask for input and suggestions.

☐ Allow for individual initiative. Don't expect the paraeducator to do things exactly the way you do them.

☐ Develop a personalized paraeducator job description for your classroom or program.

☐ Discuss how you expect the paraeducator to assist with and support classroom instruction.

☐ Establish clear supervision guidelines.

☐ Clarify any program terminology and/or jargon that might be confusing (See pages 126-143 for assistance).

Assigning Tasks

☐ Decide which tasks and duties could be delegated to a paraeducator.

☐ Prepare work assignments for paraeducators based on program needs, learning goals and objectives for students, and paraeducator's skills and experience.

☐ Consider the training, strengths and interests of paraeducators when planning schedules and assignments.

☐ Involve paraeducators in planning and organizing learning experiences based on paraeducators' qualifications and experience.

☐ Provide the paraeducator with a written list of duties and responsibilities.

☐ Organize schedules that will allow for cooperation, planning and information sharing.

☐ Discuss the paraeducator's role in any clerical duties, such as:
- ▸ Organizing classroom
- ▸ Taking attendance
- ▸ Copying materials
- ▸ Recording grades
- ▸ Ordering supplies
- ▸ Keeping records
- ▸ Collecting student work
- ▸ Grading student work
- ▸ Taking inventory of supplies
- ▸ Organizing materials
- ▸ Putting up bulletin boards
- ▸ Recording stories, lessons, and assignments

☐ If the paraeducator is working with more than one teacher, discuss how the paraeducator's time will be divided.

☐ Develop a system to monitor and observe task performance. Provide appropriate feedback.

☐ Organize work assignments to keep interruptions at a minimum.

☐ Coordinate activities with the paraeducator so that both of you can get as much done as possible.

☐ Organize and provide the materials and resources the paraeducator needs to carry out his/her assignment.

Sample Lesson or Instructional Plan

Student(s) _____ Class _____

_____ Date _____

_____ Lesson Length (time)

_____

Paraeducator_____ Supervisor_____

Objective/Goals:

Description of Activity:

Materials:

Evaluation:

After Lesson:
Note to Supervisor regarding lesson outcomes, etc.

Paraeducator Signature _____

Scheduling Paraeducator Assignments

☐ Know where, for how long, and what you want them to do.

☐ Make sure they know overall goals.

☐ Set clear objectives.

☐ Build assignments around paraeducator strengths and training.

☐ Ensure that paraeducator is clear on your instructions.

☐ Provide professional development to develop task completion skills.

☐ Seek input from the paraeducator.

☐ Set deadlines, time frames.

☐ Specify the level of authority.

☐ Guide and monitor tasks.

☐ Set up a system for feedback.

"If you are not sure where you are going, how do you tell someone else how to get there?"

—Bob Mager

Discussing Curriculum and Instruction

☐ Discuss local, state and federal guidelines that affect curriculum, instruction and assessment.

☐ Introduce the paraeducator to instructional procedures.

☐ Discuss state, local district and classroom learning goals.

☐ Explain your teaching philosophy and teaching style.

☐ Discuss your lesson plan format.

☐ Discuss relevant information regarding the Common Core State Standards (CCSS).

☐ Encourage the involvement of paraeducators in setting goals and planning, implementing and evaluating instructional activities.

☐ Share teacher guides for texts and materials.

☐ Discuss how to motivate students in the learning environment.

☐ Introduce paraeducators to classroom learning stations and explain how they are used.

☐ Allow paraeducators time to familiarize themselves with educational technology and software.

☐ Demonstrate the operation of instructional technology and audiovisual equipment.

☐ If the paraeducator is primarily assigned to one student, clarify your role in the student's instruction, including the times you will be working with the student.

☐ Discuss IEPs for students with special needs. Plan objectives and lessons that address IEP goals.

☐ Provide assistance and direction to paraeducators who work in semi-independent situations, such as:
   ▶ Job sites
   ▶ Community transition support
   ▶ Work study
   ▶ Transportation, etc.
   ▶ Computer labs
   ▶ After-school programs

☐ Support paraeducators in using modified instructional plans and materials to accommodate the learning needs of various students.

☐ Provide time for the paraeducator to share observations of students' needs and concerns with you.

Explain the paraeducator's role in:
   ▶ Drill and practice
   ▶ Testing (assessment)
   ▶ Written assignments
   ▶ Adapting or modifying curriculum
   ▶ Technology
   ▶ Monitoring student performance
   ▶ Behavior management
   ▶ Operating equipment
   ▶ Data collection
   ▶ Direct instruction

☐ Discuss the health-related needs of specific students, as appropriate.

Working with Parents and Families

☐ Discuss the paraeducator's role with parents and families of students.

☐ Discuss the importance of confidentiality and appropriate parent communication.

☐ Address the importance of respecting and listening to students and families.

☐ Discuss the paraeducator's role, if any, in parent conferences and IEP meetings.

☐ Inform parents if a paraeducator will be assisting you in instruction.

☐ Understand federal and state requirements regarding parents' "right to know" concerning staff qualifications, etc.

☐ Share information about parental rights and due process.

"Today society asks more of educators than ever before. You are required to be social workers, computer experts, juvenile officers, mediators, researchers, business partners, interdisciplinary team members and chemical dependency counselors."

— Author Unknown

Discussing Student Behavior

☐ Share district discipline policies.

☐ Discuss student accountability and expectations.

☐ Discuss time-out and school suspension policies.

☐ Discuss discipline in the classroom and your expectations for managing students' behavior. Include your views on positive reinforcement.

☐ Discuss classroom rules and regulations.

☐ Explain your practice related to students who talk during seatwork.

☐ Discuss what behavior is expected of students when they have completed an assignment.

☐ If relevant, explain student bathroom rules (permission to go, lining up, etc.)

☐ Explain out-of-seat policies.

☐ Explain your expectations for student behavior in both large and small groups.

☐ Address the importance of respecting and listening to students.

☐ Discuss positive Behavioral Intervention Plans for students with special needs.

☐ Demonstrate how to observe and chart student behavior (data collection).

☐ Train the paraeducator to observe and record student progress.

Discussing Data Collection and Student Observation

☐ Discuss the paraeducator's role in observing and recording student progress in academic areas.

☐ Discuss the paraeducator's role in observing and recording student behaviors.

☐ Discuss the paraeducator's role in observing and recording student health and safety needs.

☐ Discuss the paraeducator's role in Response to Intervention (RTI).

Discussing Student Monitoring

☐ Discuss the paraeducator's role in assisting individual students on arrival and departure.

☐ Discuss the paraeducator's role in monitoring groups of students during lunch, recess, loading/unloading busses, and hall passing periods.

☐ Discuss the paraeducator's role in providing physical proximity for students with behavior problems.

☐ Discuss the paraeducator's role in enforcing class and school rules and reinforcing appropriate social behaviors.

Promoting Training and Professional Development

☐ Explain the requirements of federal and state regulations regarding paraeducator training and qualifications.

☐ Provide paraeducators with information on district professional development opportunities.

☐ Provide opportunities for on-the-job training.

☐ Plan and provide on-the-job coaching based on the needs of the paraeducator.

☐ Develop a procedure for documenting paraeducator staff development.

☐ Discuss how training in behavior management approaches will be provided.

☐ Discuss how training in instructional approaches will be provided.

☐ Set up a mentor program for paraeducators. Arrange for veteran paraeducators to mentor beginners.

☐ Provide ongoing advocacy for the paraeducator's role in the building and district.

☐ Discuss safety issues for students.

☐ Discuss physical and medical needs of students.

☐ Discuss student behavior and rules.

☐ Discuss student academic and social needs.

☐ Provide ongoing advocacy for in-service training opportunities directly related to the daily work of paraeducators.

☐ Encourage paraeducators to participate in as much professional development as possible.

Giving Feedback

☐ Discuss the evaluation criteria that will be used by the district to assess the paraeducator's work performance.

☐ Plan a program of early observations and positive, structured support, such as mentoring.

☐ Compliment paraeducators on their contributions to the program, and let them know how much you appreciate their assistance.

☐ Provide regular, constructive feedback regarding each paraeducator's work performance.

☐ Share your plan to give paraeducators feedback on their performance. Let them know how and when feedback will be provided.

☐ When giving feedback, begin by saying what the para-educator does well, then give suggestions for improvement.

☐ Discuss formal and informal assessment and the para-educator's role in student assessment.

☐ Provide a way for both you and the paraeducator to evaluate the team relationship.

☐ Use the following checklist to provide feedback on the paraeducator's skills. Note whether each skill is well developed (WD) or needs improvement (NI).

    ____ Follows lesson as planned

    ____ Establishes rapport with students

    ____ Shows understanding of and sensitivity to student needs

    ____ Gives clear instructions to the student or group

    ____ Uses appropriate questions and cues

_____ Uses materials effectively
_____ Teaches lesson goals and objectives
_____ Keeps lesson focused on goals and objectives
_____ Keeps students on task
_____ Gives appropriate feedback to students
_____ Uses reinforcement effectively
_____ Records students' responses
_____ Stays on task and uses allotted time effectively

☐ Discuss paraeducator performance with principal when issues or concerns are noted.

The teacher is the instructional leader. Ethical and professional guidelines must be followed. Teachers who supervise paraeducators are responsible for establishing a personalized job description that includes the tasks the paraeducator will perform, where they will occur, individual student needs, materials required and instructional strategies to be used. Job descriptions should be modified as changes occur in student goals and responsibilities.

Teachers should emphasize the importance of working together as a team. A paraeducator's job is not done in isolation. A paraeducator assists and supports teacher-directed instruction (Heller & Gerlach, 2003).

"A supervisor of paraprofessionals is defined as one who knows the way, goes the way, and shows the way. They map the way by setting team goals and clarifying roles."

—Kent Gerlach

Chapter 3:
The Paraeducator's Role

Thelma is a paraeducator who has worked for the same Midwest school district for over 20 years. The district recognizes Thelma for her dedication, sense of community, teamwork and innate skills in working with students with special needs.

Each year, Thelma's responsibilities as a paraeducator have increased, and the definition of her job has expanded. Yet, she has received minimal training since beginning her career. This year Thelma is taking advantage of a statewide training program for paraeducators. Additionally, Thelma will be supervised by a first-year teacher. She has also been asked to mentor a first-year paraeducator.

What will Thelma's major responsibilities be, and what information should she share with the new paraeducator and her new supervising teacher? How can she best meet the qualifications in federal and state legislation regarding "Highly Qualified and Effective Paraprofessionals"?

Principals know *everything* about *something*.

Teachers know *something* about *everything*.

But paraeducators are expected to know *everything* about *everything* with *very little training*.

Just who are these remarkable people?

— *Author Unknown*

THE PARAEDUCATOR'S ROLE

Paraeducators play a vital role in today's classrooms. Under the supervision and management of teachers, paraeducators often prepare learning materials, assist in instructing individuals and small groups of students and work one-on-one with students with special needs.

In the past, many paraeducators received minimal training regarding their role and specific responsibilities. Paraeducators are now taking part in more staff development activities, and are recognized and respected as an integral part of the school team. As schools change, it's important for paraeducators to be proactive as they seek to clarify their roles. The following components of this checklist will serve as a valuable tool for paraeducators as they continue to meet their responsibilities and raise questions about their role in the instructional process and school community.

What Are Your Major Responsibilities?

☐ Your responsibilities as paraeducators will vary depending upon teachers' expectations, your skills and experience and job assignment. Paraeducators are primarily responsible for assisting and supporting teachers, principals and other certified or licensed staff with:

- ▶ Implementing team-based assignments.
- ▶ Building and maintaining effective communication and relationships.
- ▶ Maintaining student-centered, supportive environments.
- ▶ Organizing learning experiences for students.
- ▶ Implementing lessons initiated by the teacher or related-services personnel.
- ▶ Assessing student needs and progress under teacher direction.
- ▶ Maintaining a safe learning environment.
- ▶ Exercising good judgment, flexibility, creativity and sensitivity in response to changing situations and needs.
- ▶ Assisting in the instructional process and communicating with the teacher their perceptions of student progress and needs.
- ▶ Participating in training to develop the knowledge and skills to become a more effective paraeducator.
- ▶ Following the school policies, guidelines and procedures.
- ▶ Knowing and practicing good professional ethics.
- ▶ Using good judgment when unusual situations arise.

Learning School Policies and Procedures

☐ Make sure you know who your direct supervisor is. Supervisors may change when assignments change. You may be working with several supervisors.

☐ Make sure you know the state and local requirements for paraeducators who assist with instruction.

☐ Become familiar with school policies, guidelines and procedures—ask for them if they haven't been given to you.

☐ Obtain a copy of your job description.

☐ Make sure you understand the goals of your team and program, along with your role in helping to achieve those goals.

☐ Request the building and district mission statement. If appropriate, request the mission statement for specific programs (Title I, special education, etc.).

☐ Make sure you understand the "chain of command" in the district.

☐ Ask about any unions or affiliations you will be expected to join.

☐ Obtain information on fringe benefits, insurance, etc.

☐ Request a map of the school building. Ask for a tour if you're not familiar with the building.

☐ Request a staff directory. Exchange phone numbers with the people with who you will be directly working.

☐ Request copies of any parent or student handbooks.

☐ Request a school calendar and a schedule of special events.

☐ Request a copy of the district's discipline procedures and playground policies.

☐ Request a copy of the district's professional development calendar or inservice offerings for the year.

☐ Ask about district and community college course offerings and other professional development opportunities.

"Learn everything you can, anytime you can, from anyone you can; there will always come a time when you will be grateful you did."

—Sarah Caldwell

Questions to Ask the First Week on the Job

Your job will be a lot more manageable if you take the time to ask the following questions. Remember that asking for assistance is a strength, not a weakness!

- ☐ Is there a required orientation for my position? When will this orientation take place?
- ☐ Is a state or local district assessment required of me?
- ☐ If I'm supervised by more than one teacher, how will my time be divided? Who determines this?
- ☐ When do I meet with my supervising teacher? Is there a set time for these meetings?
- ☐ Who provides me with my weekly schedule?
- ☐ Is there a formal evaluation of my work? Who is responsible for evaluating me? Will I receive a copy of the evaluation? What will I be evaluated on?
- ☐ What is expected of me in terms of student discipline? Are there school discipline policies I should be aware of?
- ☐ What are the district's regulations regarding harassment, teasing, and bullying?
- ☐ What are the regulations for reporting child abuse and neglect?
- ☐ What are the district's regulations regarding school safety (guns, weapons, drugs, etc.)?
- ☐ Will I be assigned duties outside of the classroom (lunchroom, hallways, bus, playground, etc.)?
- ☐ When do I take my break?
- ☐ When do I have lunch?

- [ ] Am I expected to attend staff meetings? When and where are these held?

- [ ] Am I to attend parent conferences or Individualized Education Program (IEP) meetings?

- [ ] How should I respond when a parent or family member raises a question regarding a student I'm working with?

- [ ] How should I respond when a colleague asks for information about a student?

- [ ] What student and family information is available to me?

- [ ] What are the district's policies regarding confidentiality?

- [ ] What are the district's regulations regarding emergency procedures (fire drills, tornado drills, earthquake drills, lockdowns, etc.)?

- [ ] Am I expected to attend school activities such as open house, special events, etc.?

- [ ] What professional development opportunities are open to me? How will I receive information about these opportunities?

- [ ] What will be required of me in terms of professional development? How do I document my participation in this training?

- [ ] How will I receive district communication? Will I be assigned an e-mail address?

- [ ] If I am unable to work, whom should I call?

- [ ] If my supervising teacher is absent, will my role change in any way?

Working with Teachers and Other Supervisors

☐ Recognize the role of the principal as the building leader.

☐ Recognize that your supervising teacher has the primary responsibility for instructional planning and classroom management.

☐ Follow the directions and plans given to you by your principal and/or your supervising teacher.

☐ Ask clarifying questions whenever you feel the directions are not clear.

☐ Understand the distinctions between the roles of para-educators and teachers.

☐ Ask if there is a time set aside for meeting with your supervisor on a regular basis.

☐ Work under supervision within a framework of standard policies and procedures.

"To accept good advice from others is to increase ones own ability"

—*Author unknown*

Performing Assigned Tasks

☐ Ask about your role in classroom organization:
  - ▶ Obtaining, preparing and organizing instructional materials.
  - ▶ Maintaining instructional equipment.
  - ▶ Ordering materials and supplies.
  - ▶ Preparing bulletin boards, instructional and program materials, etc.
  - ▶ Organizing the learning and student environment centers.

☐ Ask about your role in building activities:
  - ▶ Monitoring the lunchroom, playground, halls or bathrooms.
  - ▶ Accompanying students to art, music, physical education and other activities.
  - ▶ Accompanying students to therapy sessions, individual appointments, job sites.
  - ▶ Accompanying students to the bus or other transportation services.
  - ▶ Complying with school safety procedures.

☐ Ask about your role regarding paperwork, clerical duties and data collection:
  - ▶ Maintaining attendance and tardy records.
  - ▶ Making copies of instructional materials.
  - ▶ Filing and organizing.
  - ▶ Collecting and recording data.
  - ▶ Recording grades, assessment results, etc.
  - ▶ Typing, word processing, and PowerPoint preparation.

- Preparing classroom or instructional materials before students arrive.
- Collecting money (books, milk, lunch, school activities, etc.).
- Grading papers and checking student work for completion.
- Taking inventory of materials and supplies.
- Ordering supplies and materials.
- Collecting student homework.
- Maintaining databases and computer-assisted instruction.
- Keeping work area clean.

"If you want to be successful, it's just this simple: Know what you're doing. Love what you're doing. And believe in what you're doing."

—O.A. Battista, Author

Supporting Curriculum and Instruction

☐ Understand the rationale, mission, philosophy and goals of the program to which you are assigned. Ask how this influences curriculum and instruction.

☐ Implement instructional strategies that are teacher developed.

☐ Implement lesson plans that are teacher designed.

☐ Assist and support teachers with individual learning activities whenever requested.

☐ Assist in the preparation of learning materials.

☐ Be aware of the methods used by teachers to accommodate a learner's needs. Assist teachers with these modifications/accommodations for students with special needs.

☐ Ask how technology is used in the classroom. Clarify your role in the use of technology. Ask for a copy of the district's internet policy.

☐ Follow the teacher's plans for strengthening students' academic and learning skills.

☐ Follow the teacher's guidelines for assessing students' academic skills.

☐ Be aware of how different learning styles effect the performance of individual students.

☐ Be aware of children's developmental patterns (cognitive, physical, social, emotional, language) at different ages. Know the factors that prohibit or impede typical development.

☐ Understand the need and requirements for learning, performance and assessment standards set by local and state educational agencies.

☐ Ask about your role in assessing and monitoring student performance.

☐ Find out how observations of student progress are to be recorded.

☐ Find out how the teacher wants you to document behavioral observations.

☐ Before beginning a lesson, ask yourself the following questions:

- ▶ Have I met with the supervising teacher concerning the goals of the lesson?
- ▶ Have I reviewed the lesson plan given to me by the teacher?
- ▶ Are the directions clear?
- ▶ Do I feel adequately prepared to assist with instruction?
- ▶ Are the teacher's objectives clear?
- ▶ Do I know how to begin the lesson?
- ▶ Do I know what to do when the student responds appropriately?
- ▶ Do I know how to handle inappropriate responses?
- ▶ Am I prepared for off-task student behavior?
- ▶ Do I have the necessary supplies and materials ready?
- ▶ Do I feel prepared to use the materials?
- ▶ Do I have the teaching area arranged efficiently?
- ▶ Is the teaching area comfortable for the student?
- ▶ Is the teaching area comfortable for me?
- ▶ Do I know how to conclude the lesson?
- ▶ Do I know how to record the results of the lesson?

☐ After the lesson is over, ask yourself the following questions:

- ▶ Have I followed the teacher's directions?
- ▶ Have I recorded instructional observations about the student?
- ▶ Have I recorded behavioral observations about the student?
- ▶ Have I completed a record or summary of the student's performance?
- ▶ How will I evaluate and communicate the results of the lesson to my supervising teacher?

☐ Prepare a substitute folder in case you are absent.

☐ Understand educational jargon and terminology. Ask for clarification if you don't know or understand a term. (Use pages 126-143 to help with this).

> "You must provide for children who don't speak English; who are gifted learners, visual learners, kinesthetic learners, voracious learners, and reluctant learners; who have behavior problems, are hungry and/or homeless. We ask you to teach children how to drive, get along with others, balance a checkbook, make healthy choices, use new technologies— and, yes, how to read, write, and do arithmetic."
>
> —Author Unknown

Dealing with Student Behavior

☐ Understand district policy and procedural safeguards regarding the behavior management and discipline of students.

☐ Implement student behavioral plans that have been designed by certified or licensed staff.

☐ Understand effective strategies for dealing with verbal aggression and other forms of resistance.

☐ Ask about your role in:

- ▶ Observing and charting student behavior.

- ▶ Correcting student behavior.

- ▶ Enforcing school, program, and class rules.

- ▶ Assisting students with interpersonal problem solving and conflict resolution.

- ▶ Overseeing student activities.

- ▶ Completing required discipline documentation.

- ▶ Assisting in crisis intervention.

- ▶ Maintaining school and classroom safety.

- ▶ Implementing behavior plans.

☐ Ask questions about the behavior management strategies used by each teacher you work with. Teachers may have different approaches to behavior management and reinforcement. Paraeducators should follow the behavior management strategies of the supervising teacher.

☐ Reinforce appropriate student behavior as modeled by the teacher and record accurate data when necessary.

Assisting Students with Special Needs

☐ Request a copy of the state or district guidelines for parents of children with special needs (due process, parental rights, etc.).

☐ Request general disability and/or health information if you do not understand the characteristics of the disability or health issue.

☐ Understand the roles of related services personnel, such as physical and occupational therapists, speech and language pathologists and school nurses in delivering services to students and families.

☐ Ask about your role in:
  ▶ Attending parent/family conferences.
  ▶ Communicating relevant information, observations and insights about students to other team members.
  ▶ Attending or providing input for IEP meetings.
  ▶ Working with related services personnel and other team members.
  ▶ Assisting with accommodations and curriculum modifications.
  ▶ Implementing Behavioral Intervention Plans (BIPs).
  ▶ Monitoring and documenting student progress toward IEP goals.
  ▶ Obtaining services for students.
  ▶ Reporting suspected child abuse and neglect.
  ▶ Informing staff regarding emotional needs of students.
  ▶ Assisting with transition services and plans.
  ▶ Supporting family service plans.

- ▸ Performing emergency procedures and participating in safety drills.
- ▸ Responding to medically related needs of students.
- ▸ Administering medication to students.
- ▸ Providing personal physical care to students.
- ▸ Instructing students in personal hygiene and safety practices.
- ▸ Monitoring physical environment for safety and correcting unsafe conditions where possible.
- ▸ Communicating with parents and families of children with special needs. (Check school or district policy.)
- ▸ Respecting the rights of the student and parents to the least restrictive environment.
- ▸ Modeling age-appropriate behavior.
- ▸ Collaborating and communicating with other educational personnel on policies, laws and issues regarding students in special education programs.
- ▸ Educating others regarding students with special needs.
- ▸ Encouraging student independence.

☐ Follow and use universal health precautions for preventing illnesses and infections; follow and use proper procedures for lifting students and heavy objects.

☐ Follow the confidentiality policies of the district.

☐ Exercise prudent judgment regarding the safety and welfare of students.

What You Need to Know About a Student's Individualized Education Program (IEP)

An IEP is a legal plan written by a team of professionals that documents the learning priorities for the school year.

Every IEP must legally include the following information:

▸ Present levels of performance (how the student is performing across subject areas).

▸ Measurable goals and objectives (this indicates the annual goals for a student across subject areas).

▸ Special education and related services (this is the type, level and amount of service that will be provided by special education staff).

▸ The extent of participation with children without disabilities.

▸ A statement of how a student's progress will be measured (the team needs to describe how often a student's progress will be measured).

▸ Modifications (the student's modifications or adaptations must be listed).

▸ Participation in statewide tests (the IEP indicates whether the student will participate in statewide tests and if so, what modifications will be provided).

▸ Times/locations of services to be provided (this explains the amount of time student's will receive services and the location, e.g., general education classroom).

What paraeducators need to know:

- [ ] Paraeducators must understand that the information within the IEP document is confidential and cannot be shared with anyone outside the student's IEP team.

- [ ] Paraeducators may or may not be asked to participate in an IEP meeting. Your district may have guidelines for this.

- [ ] If you do not attend the meeting, ask your supervisor to summarize the IEP meeting.

- [ ] Paraeducators need to know the goals and objectives for the student.

"Education is learning what you didn't even know you didn't know."

—Daniel Boorstin, Author, Historian

Obtaining Training and Professional Development

☐ Ask what staff development will be required of you.

☐ Ask how your training—workshops, etc.—should be documented. Find out who maintains this documentation.

☐ Ask about the district career ladder program.

☐ Accept responsibility for improving your skills.

☐ Obtain training to meet the needs of students as required by their IEPs.

☐ Request state and district staff development policies or plans for paraeducators.

☐ Request a list of training opportunities in the local area, such as community college programs, district training opportunities, state educational agency training, etc. that is available to you.

☐ Find out the state requirements for meeting the para-professional "Highly Qualified" standards and qualifications in federal legislation.

☐ Ask if any state or local assessments will be required of you. Find out when and where these assessments are given.

☐ Show a positive attitude toward self-improvement.

Maintaining Ethical Conduct and Professionalism

☐ Maintain your own wellness, composure and emotional stability while working with students and staff.

☐ Always present yourself as a positive role model for students. Represent the school district or agency in a positive manner.

☐ Share relevant information with other team members to facilitate problem solving, program planning and student concerns.

☐ Participate in regularly scheduled staff meetings as requested.

☐ Understand the value of a team approach to the delivery of instructional services.

☐ Follow the directions of the supervising teacher and other licensed or certificated staff.

☐ Provide accurate information about students to those who need the information (e.g., supervising teacher, related services personnel, school counselor, and other staff).

☐ Discuss confidential school and student issues only with appropriate school personnel.

☐ If you have concerns about a staff member, discuss those concerns directly with that person.

☐ Follow the chain of command established by the school district to address policy questions, system issues and personnel practices.

☐ Discuss a student's progress or educational program only with the teachers or staff responsible for that student's instruction.

- [ ] Refer concerns expressed by parents, students and other staff to your supervising teacher or principal.
- [ ] When you feel problems cannot be resolved by you and the team, use the district grievance procedures. Make sure you understand those procedures.
- [ ] Respect the legal and human rights of children and youth.
- [ ] Respect parental rights.
- [ ] Follow the ethical guidelines of professional organizations.
- [ ] Practice the standards of professional and ethical conduct approved by the school or agency.
- [ ] Recognize and respect the roles of teachers as supervisors and team leaders.
- [ ] Participate in continuing staff development and self-improvement.
- [ ] Know school policies and procedures.
- [ ] Arrive promptly and follow the daily schedule.
- [ ] Dress appropriately.
- [ ] Manage time efficiently during the work day.
- [ ] Model the teaching and behavior management techniques demonstrated by the teacher.

Chapter 4:
The Principal's Role

Frank is a principal in a growing West Coast school district. He supervises 19 teachers, 12 paraeducators, and 12 other education support professionals. Many of the paraeducators work with students in special education, Title I or bilingual programs. Some of the paraeducators were parent volunteers before they were hired.

Frank knows that the paraeducators in his school play an increasingly important role in instruction. Frank, however, does not fully understand his role in paraeducator supervision. "I used to leave the directing of the work of paraeducators to the teacher, but I know I have major responsibilities also," he acknowledges.

This year Frank has been asked by the district to delineate the role principals play in paraeducator employment, supervision and training. What should Frank tell them? What are a principal's major responsibilities and what steps should he or she take to create an effective school tem? How will the district respond to recent federal and state legislation regarding appropriate training and supervision of paraeducators? How will the district recruit and retain paraeducators? How will the district paraeducators meet the "highly qualified" standards and qualifications set by the federal government and the state?

THE PRINCIPAL'S ROLE

The principal and other school administrators are critical to the success of instructional teams. The principal takes the leadership role in creating a school climate in which paraeducators have a professional identity and contribute to activities that help to enhance student achievement. Even though teachers are responsible for the day-to-day instructional supervision of paraeducators, principals are responsible for the administrative supervision, which includes the interviewing, hiring, preparation, evaluation and dismissal of paraeducators. The following checklist will serve as a guide for administrators who want to improve the effectiveness of paraeducators and the teachers who direct their work. They will answer questions such as:

> ‣ What are my major responsibilities?
> ‣ What do I need to know about recruiting and hiring paraeducators?
> ‣ What do I need to do to create a professional climate?
> ‣ What do I need to include in a job description?
> ‣ What is my role in providing a building and job orientation?
> ‣ How do I share school policies and procedures?
> ‣ How do I support the teacher-paraeducator team?
> ‣ How do I evaluate a paraeducator's performance?
> ‣ How do I provide staff development?

What Are Your Major Responsibilities?

The principal and/or other school administrators have the responsibility for:

▶ Recruiting, interviewing and hiring paraeducators.

▶ Providing an environment and a scheduling time during which effective communication, teamwork and planning with the supervising teacher and para-educator may occur.

▶ Making sure that all new and returning teachers understand their role in the supervision of para-educators.

▶ Assisting in providing district-level and building-level orientation to new and returning paraeducators.

▶ Assigning paraeducators to specific programs, teachers, classrooms or educational teams.

▶ Working with Human Resources to develop appro-priate job descriptions.

▶ Providing support that will help team members resolve interpersonal or other problems in class-rooms or other learning environments.

▶ Developing appropriate policies for the employment, training and supervision of paraeducators.

▶ Evaluating paraeducators and their supervising teachers.

▶ Promoting effective teamwork in the building and within teacher-paraeducator teams.

▶ Developing and disseminating written safety proce-dures and policies for all types of instructional programming.

- Providing professional development opportunities for paraeducators and those who supervise them.
- Providing leadership in support of effective teamwork.
- Documenting the training requirements of paraeducators.
- Following federal and state guidelines regarding paraeducator qualifications.
- Making sure teachers understand their role as instructional supervisors.

An Effective Team Leader

- Understands and is committed to TEAM goals.
- Is friendly, concerned, and interested in others.
- Acknowledges and confronts conflict openly.
- Listens to others with understanding.
- Includes others in the decision-making process.
- Contributes ideas and solutions.
- Values the ideas and contributions of others.
- Recognizes and rewards team efforts.
- Encourages and appreciates comments about team performance.

Recruiting and Hiring Paraeducators

Too often job expectations for paraeducators are vague, misleading and even inappropriate. A clear job description will clarify the roles of the paraeducator in the school program and help the principal start the hiring process on a solid footing.

☐ Work with Human Resources personnel to improve job descriptions for paraeducators. The job description should clarify the role of the paraeducator in the education program.

☐ Make sure Human Resources personnel understand the state and federal qualification requirements for paraeducators who work in Title I schools, special education and other assignments.

☐ Be an advocate for paraeducators.

☐ Advocate for appropriate teacher training and certification.

☐ Advocate for appropriate training for paraeducators.

☐ Make sure all teachers who supervise paraeducators have training in supervising and directing the work of paraeducators. Include that content in new teacher orientation.

☐ Make the district school board aware of the role paraeducators play in your building, as well as the state and federal guidelines regarding their role.

☐ Consult with all necessary personnel (including teachers and paraeducators) in the development of the paraeducator job description and staff development plans.

☐ Use district-level job descriptions to provide the foundation for school-generated job descriptions. Job descriptions for paraeducators should include the following:

- ▶ Job title that is specific to the job
- ▶ Position setting
- ▶ Qualifications
- ▶ Purpose for the position
- ▶ Professional development requirements
- ▶ Details regarding specific duties and role responsibilities
- ▶ Hours of employment, salary, fringe benefits
- ▶ Supervision guidelines and responsibilities

☐ Include the supervising teacher in the paraeducator job interview whenever possible.

☐ Share the district and school mission statements with the job candidate in the interview.

☐ Explain the fringe benefits package in the interview, if applicable.

☐ If payroll and benefits are explained at the district level, check for the paraeducator's understanding. Provide sufficient information for the new paraeducator regarding benefits.

☐ Formulate interview questions for paraeducators such as the following:
- ▶ Why do you want to work at this school and in the district?
- ▶ Why do you want to work with children?
- ▶ What is your previous work experience and specific work experience with children?
- ▶ What are your long-range career goals?
- ▶ What personal qualities and skills can you offer students, teachers and the school?
- ▶ What is your understanding of the practice of inclusion?

- Do you have hobbies and/or interests that might contribute to job performance?
- What is your definition of "paraeducator," "instructional assistant," or whatever term is used in your district?
- How do you feel about possibly being supervised by more than one person?
- What training have you had to meet district requirements for paraprofessionals?
- Do you know what additional training is required to meet local, state and federal guidelines (IDEA, ESEA requirements)?
- Do you understand the legal and professional issues regarding the employment, supervision and training of paraeducators?

☐ Formulate interview questions for teacher candidates who might supervise paraprofessionals, such as the following:
- What do you see as the main responsibilities of a supervisor of paraeducators?
- How comfortable are you directing and managing the work of paraeducators?
- Have you ever supervised adults in a work setting?
- What are some of the duties you would assign a paraeducator?
- How do you see the paraeducator role in the classroom?
- Did your student teaching or internship experience provide any opportunity to work with paraeducators?

Good Job Descriptions are Important

A job description is a formalized statement of the duties, qualifications and responsibilities of a job based on information obtained through an objective job analysis. Its purpose is to identify a specific job with clarity and precision and to describe its scope and content. It may include information on working conditions, tools, equipment used, knowledge and skills needed to do the job, and relationships with other positions and employees. It should be accurate, concise and complete.

Job descriptions clarify who is responsible for certain tasks, and help the employee understand the specific responsibilities of the position. Job descriptions are also helpful to applicants, supervisors and personnel staff at every stage in the employment relationship. Accurate job descriptions are a prerequisite for accurate and meaningful evaluations, wage and salary surveys and an equitable wage and salary structure.

"Effective teaching may be the hardest job there is."

—William Glasser

Basic Elements of a Good Job Description

Job Identification

☐ What is the job title?

☐ In what department is the job located?

☐ What is the title of the supervisor to whom the employee will report?

☐ Does the employee supervise other employees? If so, give their job titles and a brief description of their responsibilities.

Job Summary

☐ A brief but informative narrative of the position. This information should be general in nature but still provide the reader with an understanding of the overall description of the position, job goals and a general portrayal of the kind of individual who would be best suited for this position.

Job Duties

☐ What duties must be regularly performed by the employee? List them in their order of importance and, if possible, indicate the approximate percentage of time for each duty.

☐ Does the employee perform other duties periodically? If so, list these tasks and, if possible, indicate the frequency.

☐ Describe the everyday tasks of the job in terms of variety and complexity. How will information be obtained, interpreted and used by the employee?

Job Specifications

- ☐ How much education, experience, and training is necessary in order to perform the job satisfactorily?
- ☐ What professional development, if any, is expected?
- ☐ What are the working conditions? Be specific about noise, heat/cold, space, repetitious work, degree of supervision, etc. Include mental, physical and environmental demands.
- ☐ What machines, tools, equipment is the employee responsible for maintaining, safekeeping and operating?

Accountabilities

- ☐ At what point is the employee's performance reviewed?
- ☐ What additional training or education will be required? When and how often?
- ☐ Use team language.
- ☐ Make sure paraeducator job description states "under supervision," or "under direction."

Creating a Professional Climate

☐ Take a leadership role in creating a school climate in which paraeducators have a professional identity.

☐ Provide an atmosphere of respect, recognition and open communication.

☐ Make sure new paraeducators are introduced to all building staff.

☐ Develop standards for assigning paraeducators to jobs for which they are qualified or have the appropriate skills.

☐ Appoint paraeducators to school-based teams and committees whenever possible. (Paraeducators are often not represented on school committees, even though their input is valuable.)

☐ Provide a common planning time for team members. Teachers should have time in their schedules to communicate with paraeducators.

☐ Make sure that newsletters, staff development activities and other district communications include information for and about paraeducators.

☐ Inform parents and families about the role of para-educators in the implementation of their child's program. This is especially important in special education and Title I programs.

☐ Inform the superintendent and school board about the positive work of paraeducators in the district.

☐ Work closely with the directors of special education, Title I and other special programs on specific para-educator roles and responsibilities.

Providing Building and Job Orientation

☐ Prepare a list of terms frequently used in the building that may need a definition or explanation, such as Title I, IEP (Individualized Education Program), LD (learning disability), BD (behavior disorder), etc. Material included at the end of this book may be helpful in this activity. (See pages 126-143).

☐ Make sure paraeducators know their role is to assist and support teacher-directed instruction.

☐ Make sure newly hired paraeducators know some basic building information, such as:
  ▶ Parking availability
  ▶ Location of staff restrooms
  ▶ Location of staff lounge
  ▶ Scheduling for staff breaks and lunch
  ▶ Bus system
  ▶ Student demographics—describe any recent changes
  ▶ Location of stored materials and procedures for obtaining them
  ▶ Office procedures
  ▶ Lunchroom procedures

☐ Appoint a committee to design a building-based handbook for paraeducators. The handbook could contain the following:
  ▶ Paraeducator definition
  ▶ Map of building
  ▶ Phone numbers of faculty and staff
  ▶ Emergency procedures (fire drill, tornado, earthquake, etc.)

- ▶ Job descriptions
- ▶ Chain of command (organizational structure)
- ▶ Staff development opportunities
- ▶ Supervision policy
- ▶ Evaluation criteria
- ▶ Appeal/grievance procedures
- ▶ District policies (confidentiality, etc.)
- ▶ Discipline procedures (playground rules, cafeteria rules, etc.)
- ▶ Procedures to report child abuse and neglect
- ▶ School calendar
- ▶ Procedures for substitutes
- ▶ Person to call if ill or absent
- ▶ School schedules (daily and weekly schedules, meeting schedules, etc.)
- ▶ Other items specific to school activities
- ▶ District reporting forms

☐ Make sure paraeducators are comfortable with tasks assigned to them.

☐ Make sure paraeducators know that asking for assistance is a strength, not a weakness. Invite their questions, and meet with them regularly.

> *"Statistics show that turnover is less,*
> *the more training employees get:*
> *Interest in their development*
> *seems to inspire loyalty."*
>
> —Tom Peters, *"Success Magazine"*
> March, 1988

Sharing School Policies and Procedures

☐ Share with paraeducators any state and federal policies regarding their role: IDEA and ESEA.

☐ Give paraeducators any district policies on the rights of parents, especially those related to students with disabilities.

☐ Share the district and building mission statements with paraeducators.

☐ Set up a procedure to ensure that paraeducators receive important building and district communications. (Provide them with an email address.)

☐ Give paraeducators copies of student and parent handbooks.

☐ Make sure paraeducators are informed if they are to attend staff meetings. If this is not a requirement, make sure they receive minutes of the meeting or a summary of the issues discussed that could affect them.

☐ Introduce paraeducators to professional organizations.

☐ Introduce paraeducators to the district/state code of conduct for educational professionals.

☐ Give paraeducators copies of state assessment requirements, such as:

  ▶ Learning goals
  ▶ Legislation and policy statements that affect their role
  ▶ Special education referral and prereferral process
  ▶ Procedures for fire drills and school crisis plans
  ▶ Special education policy, including information on the rights of parents and families

- ▶ Title I policy
- ▶ Bilingual program policies
- ▶ Child abuse and neglect reporting guidelines

☐ Share the district evaluation process with paraeducators, teachers, and other licensed staff.

☐ Explain how email as well as classroom and school web sites are used as communication tools.

☐ Distribute district internet policies.

Supporting the Teacher-Paraeducator Team

☐ Make sure paraeducators have clearly defined roles and that these roles have been communicated to all para-educators and their supervising teachers.

☐ Meet with all new teachers to make sure they under-stand their responsibilities in directing the work of para-educators. Make sure teachers have a clearly defined role in supervision.

☐ Make sure paraeducators and teachers have the skill necessary for effective teamwork and communication.

☐ Help paraeducators understand who the supervisor is for each assignment and the role of that supervisor in directing and managing their work.

☐ Build a time in the schedule for paraeducators and teachers to communicate and plan together.

☐ Hold meetings with all building-level paraeducators at least monthly.

Providing Training and Professional Development

☐ Determine what local, state, federal and other legal mandates exist for paraeducator staff development and supervision.

☐ Assess emerging training needs for teachers and para-educators.

☐ Design a professional development plan for paraeduca-tors.

☐ Offer a variety of options for supporting and preparing paraeducators, including:
  ▸ Support groups   ▸ Mentorships
  ▸ Study teams   ▸ Web site information
  ▸ Opportunities to be members of a professional organization at the local, state, or national level
  ▸ Information about local union membership
  ▸ Information about state- and district-required training and staff development
  ▸ Regional or state conferences
  ▸ Assessment information

☐ Invite paraeducators to relevant staff development activities and conferences offered to teachers—encourage partnerships, with the teacher and paraeducator attending as a team.

☐ Provide time and resources for staff development before paraeducators begin their assignment and ongoing staff development thereafter.

☐ Collaborate with other districts to cohost training oppor-tunities or a regional conference.

☐ Determine how paraeducators are being utilized in the building and district.

☐ Take time to observe paraeducators on a regular basis.

☐ Schedule opportunities for teachers and paraeducators to meet regularly for on-the-job training, planning, and communication.

☐ Develop a needs assessment instrument for training and an evaluation for staff development.

☐ Assess prior staff development activities and community college resources.

☐ Determine what incentives are needed for paraeducator staff development:

- ▶ Salary scale
- ▶ Stipends
- ▶ Professional credit units
- ▶ Release time
- ▶ Career ladder opportunities
- ▶ Training materials

☐ Arrange for "parasubstitutes" if professional development is scheduled during the workday.

☐ Ensure that paraeducators are trained properly to respond to emergencies and school safety issues.

☐ Make paraeducators aware of career ladder programs that could lead to teacher certification.

☐ Develop workshops for teachers and administrators on how to work effectively with paraeducators, including the following areas:

- ▶ Providing feedback
- ▶ Mentoring strategies
- ▶ Supervision guidelines
- ▶ Evaluation guidelines
- ▶ Planning and scheduling
- ▶ New legislation
- ▶ Roles and responsibilities of team members
- ▶ Classroom and behavior management
- ▶ Professionalism and ethics
- ▶ Communication and team building

- ▶ Directing and managing the work of paraeducators
- ▶ Characteristics of adult learners
- ▶ On-the-job training and coaching
- ▶ Interpersonal problem solving

☐ Consider workshops for paraeducators on how to work effectively with students, including the following areas:

- ▶ Confidentiality issues
- ▶ Instructional strategies
- ▶ Data collection
- ▶ Conflict resolution
- ▶ Basic technology skills
- ▶ Special education
- ▶ Professionalism and ethics
- ▶ Bullying and teasing
- ▶ Roles and responsibilities of team members
- ▶ Behavior management and discipline
- ▶ Basic understanding of specific disabilities
- ▶ Inclusion and special education
- ▶ Diversity issues, including cultural issues
- ▶ Stress management/wellness issues
- ▶ Child development and developmentally appropriate practice
- ▶ Specialty care: lifting, back care, etc.
- ▶ Reporting of child abuse and neglect
- ▶ First aid, CPR, and handling emergency situations
- ▶ Legal and human rights of children
- ▶ Communication and team building
- ▶ Assisting with reading and math instruction
- ▶ Understanding the Common Core State Standards (CCSS)
- ▶ Instructional programming
- ▶ State and federal legislation and guidelines
- ▶ State assessment requirements
- ▶ Response to Intervention (RTI)

Evaluation of Paraeducator Training

☐ Have knowledge and skills required by paraeducators and assistants to work in different positions and programs and across disciplines, been identified and developed?

☐ Are there systematic competency-based opportunities for personnel development and career advancement?
  ▶ For paraeducators
  ▶ For teachers and administrators who supervise paraeducators
  ▶ For educators and other professionals who direct the work of paraeducators

☐ Does the training content provide paraeducators and their supervisors with an understanding of the roles of professionals as team leaders, diagnosticians, program planners and supervisors of paraeducators?

☐ Have the team leadership and supervisory roles been identified and the knowledge and skill competencies developed to prepare the professionals for those roles?

☐ Does the training content demonstrate respect for children and youth with disabilities and their families, as well as for those who come from diverse ethnic, cultural and language backgrounds?

☐ Does the training content include information on the ethical, legal and team-based roles of professionals and paraeducators in the delivery of education and related services?

☐ Do licensed/certified professionals involved in the training of paraeducators have knowledge of and respect for the distinction between professional and paraeducator roles?

☐ Is sufficient time and opportunity provided for orientation, initial training, and continued competency development?

☐ How can different constituencies (e.g., professional associations and provider agencies) contribute to efforts to improve the quality of teacher/paraeducator staff development?

Evaluating Paraeducators and the Teachers Who Supervise Them

☐ Provide leadership in the evaluation and systematic improvement of teacher supervision and monitoring of paraeducators.

☐ Develop, in collaboration with teachers, performance indicators and instruments for assessing the performance of paraeducators and guidelines for involving teachers in the annual performance reviews of paraeducators.

☐ Explain the evaluation system for both teachers and paraeducators by reviewing the process and criteria.

End of the Year Program Evaluation

☐ Provide clear guidelines for evaluation and supervision.

Sample Evaluation Checklist

☐ Works cooperatively with peers.

☐ Participates in school activities as appropriate for a staff member.

☐ Performs duties and assignments effectively under the direction of the classroom teacher.

☐ Participates in activities to promote general welfare of the school and improved teaching and learning.

☐ Maintains professional appearance and demeanor.

☐ Maintains regular attendance in conformity with rules and regulations of the school district.

☐ Assists the classroom teacher with establishing and maintaining a challenging teaching/learning environment.

☐ Assists the classroom teacher with the provision of instructional activities at the appropriate level for all students.

☐ Assists the classroom teacher with establishing and maintaining appropriate management procedures in the class.

☐ Assists the classroom teacher with the creation of an environment in which students work with a sense of purpose and understand what is expected of them.

☐ Treats students with fairness, respect and consistency.

☐ Plans lessons for small group instruction at the direction of the teacher.

- [ ] Uses materials related to the objectives of lesson at the direction of the teacher.
- [ ] Follows lesson plan and presents it clearly and logically.
- [ ] Engages in activities that contribute to one's performance in the teaching/learning situation.
- [ ] Responds to in-service and professional growth opportunities in terms of personal and pupil improvement).

"It is not knowledge, but the act of learning, not possession but the act of getting there, which grants the greatest enjoyment."

—Carl Friedrich Gauss

Guiding Principles for Paraeducator Employment, Roles, Preparation and Supervision*

Using a 3-point scale, where 1 is Fully Developed and 3 is Not Yet Evident, indicate under Rating the presence of this principle in your building or district. Use Comment section to indicate any action needed or significant factors.

	Rating	Comments
Guiding Principle 1: Skilled paraeducators are employed to improve the quality of education and services in other provider systems and to help ensure supportive, inclusive, safe, and healthy learning environments for children, youth, and staff.		
Guiding Principle 2: Administrators and teachers/providers create environments that recognize paraeducators as valued team members and effectively integrate them into teams.		
Guiding Principle 3: Members of all program planning and implementation teams participate within clearly defined roles in changing, dynamic environments to provide learner-centered and individualized experiences and services for all children and youth and their families.		
Guiding Principle 4: Paraeducators are respected and supported in their team roles by policymakers, administrators, teachers/providers, and families.		

	Rating	Comments
Guiding Principle 5: Standards for paraeducator roles and professional development assure that they are assigned to positions for which they are qualified and have the skills required to assist teachers/providers to provide quality learning experiences and related services for all children and youth and their families.		
Guiding Principle 6: Paraeducators receive pre- and in-service professional development provided by the district/agency and opportunities for continuing education or career advancement offered by institutions of higher education.		
Guiding Principle 7: Teachers/providers responsible for supervising the work of paraeducators have the skills necessary to plan for, direct, provide on-the-job training for, monitor, and evaluate the performance of paraeducators.		
Guiding Principle 8: Paraeducators have an occupational/professional identity and contribute to learner-centered activities that help to achieve the mission of the school/agency.		

*These guiding principles are based on research activities conducted by the National Resource Center for Paraeducators and paraeducator development efforts in Utah, Minnesota, Iowa, Washington, and Rhode Island.

District and/or Building Assessment of Paraeducator Issues

Put a check in the box that best describes your district or building current status. Make any additional comments for *Action Needed* on page 118, the last page of this chart.

A. Policy Development and Paraeducator Acknowledgement Guidelines* *Underline the term used in your district (paraprofessional, instructional assistant, educational assistant, other: _____)	Developed	Not Sure	Needs Improvement
The state and local district have defined the term "paraeducator."			
Paraeducators provide services under the direct supervision of certified teachers, administrators or licensed personnel.			
State policy exists regarding paraeducator qualifications and supervision guidelines.			
Local district policy exists regarding paraeducator qualifications and supervision guidelines.			
Skilled paraeducators are employed to improve the quality of education and services.			
Paraeducators help ensure supportive, inclusive, safe and healthy learning environments for children, youth and staff.			
Paraeducators have an occupational/professional identity and contribute to learner-centered activities that help to achieve the mission of the school/agency.			
Administrators and teachers create environments that recognize paraeducators as valued team members and effectively integrate them into teams.			
Paraeducators are valued, respected, appreciated and recognized for their unique competencies and contributions to the school, community and classroom.			
A district handbook for paraeducators exists.			

District and/or Building Assessment of Paraeducator Issues

Put a check in the box that best describes your district or building current status. Make any additional comments for *Action Needed* on page 118, the last page of this chart.

B. Hiring and Assignment of Paraeducators	Developed	Not Sure	Needs Improvement
The district has an agreed upon process and criteria for determining whether paraeducator's support is needed to assist the teacher in delivering instruction.			
Paraeducators have a job description that outlines their roles and responsibilities.			
Supervising teachers have job descriptions that outline their role in directing and managing the work of paraeducators.			
When paraeducator support is determined to be necessary, a written plan exists that clarifies the nature and extent of the support.			
In most circumstances it is advisable to assign paraeducators to classrooms or instructional programs rather than to an individual student. In cases when a paraeducator is needed for an individual student, efforts are made to ensure that paraeducators provide supportive rather than primary or exclusive services.			
Substitute paraeducators are recruited and trained to ensure that a student's access to education and participation in his/her educational program is not unduly disrupted when the regular paraeducator is unavailable.			

District and/or Building Assessment of Paraeducator Issues

Put a check in the box that best describes your district or building current status. Make any additional comments for *Action Needed* on page 118, the last page of this chart.

C. Orientation and Training of Paraeducators	Developed	Not Sure	Needs Improvement
Paraeducators receive orientation and entry-level training prior to working directly with students.			
Paraeducators receive ongoing, on-the-job training to match their specific job responsibilities and assignments.			
Paraeducators have access to ongoing professional development, in addition to their on-the-job experiences.			
Standards for paraeducator roles and professional development assure that they are assigned to positions for which they are qualified. They have the skills required to assist teachers/providers to provide quality learning experiences and related services for all children, youth and their families.			
Paraeducators receive pre-service and in-service professional development. Opportunities exist for continuing education or career advancement.			
Paraeducators working with students with special needs receive information regarding the student's disability and IEP goals.			

District and/or Building Assessment of Paraeducator Issues			
Put a check in the box that best describes your district or building current status. Make any additional comments for *Action Needed* on page 118, the last page of this chart.			
D. Paraeducator Interactions with Students and Staff (evaluation)	Developed	Not Sure	Needs Improvement
An up-to-date district paraeducator performance evaluation instrument has been developed.			
A system to evaluate and give feedback to paraeducators has been established.			
When administrators are making work assignments and reassignments to meet students' educational needs, input is solicited directly from paraeducators, teachers and other team members to understand factors that may influence job performance.			
Paraeducators are expected to demonstrate constructive interpersonal skills with students and other team members.			
Paraeducators develop and demonstrate attitudes and work habits that encourage student independence, foster appropriate interdependence, promote inclusion and peer interactions and enhance each students' self-image.			

District and/or Building Assessment of Paraeducator Issues

Put a check in the box that best describes your district or building current status. Make any additional comments for *Action Needed* on page 118, the last page of this chart.

E. Roles and Responsibilities of Paraeducators	Developed	Not Sure	Needs Improvement
Administrators, teachers and related service providers have the ultimate responsibility for ensuring the appropriate design, implementation and evaluation of instruction carried out by paraeducators.			
Paraeducators function as vital support to students under the direction of certificated teachers or administrators.			
Some functions of paraeducators are to: assist/support in the implementation of instructional programs; facilitate learning activities; collect data; and carry out other assigned duties based on plans developed by the supervising teacher.			
Paraeducators are informed about educational needs and characteristics of the students with whom they work, as well as classroom, school policies, practices and schedules.			
Paraeducators have opportunities to contribute to the development of the educational program, education plans and activities created by each student's educational team.			
Members of all program planning and implementation teams participate within clearly defined roles in changing, dynamic environments to provide learner-centered and individualized experiences and services for all children and youth and their families.			
Communication time is scheduled daily or weekly to allow opportunities for paraeducators to be oriented to teacher's plans, report on student progress, ask questions and offer input.			

District and/or Building Assessment of Paraeducator Issues

Put a check in the box that best describes your district or building current status. Make any additional comments for *Action Needed* on page 118, the last page of this chart.

F. Supervision and Evaluation of Paraeducator Services	Developed	Not Sure	Needs Improvement
Supervisors of paraeducators (teachers and administrators) receive training in effective supervisory practices and ethical and legal issues concerning paraeducator roles and responsibilities.			
Teachers, principals and other licensed personnel responsible for supervising the work of paraeducators have the skills necessary to plan for, direct, provide on-the-job training, monitor and evaluate the performance of paraeducators.			
Paraeducators receive ongoing supervision and regular performance evaluations which are based on their job descriptions.			
When an individual student is receiving support from a paraeducator, an evaluation plan is established to determine how and when paraeducator services can be faded out through increased student independence or replaced by more naturally occurring supports.			
In inclusion programs, the special education teacher, general education teacher, and paraeducator meet regularly to discuss their roles and responsibilities.			

Adapted from: Giangreco, M. F., Edelman, S., & Broer, S. (June 2001). *A guide to schoolwide planning for paraeducator supports.* Burlington, VT: University of Vermont, Center on Disability and Community Inclusion. Retrieved from: www.uvm.edu/~cdci/parasupport/guide.html

Action Needed Items

List any other relevant information you have or need to obtain. If you checked "not sure" for any of the assessment questions, who do you need to ask to obtain the information?

_____

_____

_____

_____

_____

_____

_____

_____

Resources

Print and Video

Chopra, R.V. & N.K. French. Paraeducator Relationships with Parents of Students with Significant Disabilities. *Remedial and Special Education,* 25(4) 240-251, 2004.

French, Nancy. *Guide to the Supervision of Paraeducators* (laminated reference guide). Port Chester, NY: National Professional Resources, Inc., 2007.

French, Nancy. Managing paraeducators. In *Supervising Paraeducators in Educational Settings: A Team Approach,* edited by A.L. Pickett & K. Gerlach. Austin, TX: Pro-Ed, Inc., 2nd Edition, 2003.

French, N.K. *Managing Paraeducators in your School.* Thousand Oaks, CA: Corwin Press, 2003.

French, Nancy. Paraeducators in special education programs. *Focus on Exceptional Children,* (36) 2, 1-16, October, 2003.

French, Nancy. *Paraeducators: Quality Supervision and Training* (DVD). Port Chester, NY: National Professional Resources, Inc., 2009.

French, Nancy. *Paraeducators Resource Guide* (laminated reference guide). Port Chester, NY: National Professional Resources, Inc., 2013.

Friend, M. & Cook. *Introductions: Collaborative Skills for School Professionals.* Boston, MA: Pearson Education, 2003.

Gerlach, Kent. *The Paraeducator and Teacher Team: Strategies for Success—Roles, Responsibilities, and Ethical Issues.* Seattle, WA: Pacific Training Associates, 2014.

Gerlach, Kent. *The Paraeducator and Teacher Team: Strategies for Success—Communication and Team Building.* Seattle, WA: Pacific Training Associates, 8th Edition, 2014.

Gerlach, Kent. *The Paraeducator and Teacher Team: Strategies for Success—Time Management for Teams.* Seattle, WA: Pacific Training Associates, 6th Edition, 2014.

Gerlach, Kent. *The Paraeducator and Teacher Team: Strategies for Success—Paraeducator Supervision.* Seattle, WA: Pacific Training Associates, 11th Edition, 2014.

Giangreco, Michael, Susan Edelman & Stephen Brown. *A Guide to Schoolwide Planning for Paraeducator Supports.* Center on Disability and Community Inclusion, University of Vermont, June 2001.

Giangreco, Michael, Susan Edelman & Stephen Broer. Schoolwide Planning to Improve Paraeducator Supports. *Exceptional Children,* Vol. 70, 2003.

Giangreco, Michael, Susan Edelman, T. E. Luiselli, & MacFarland. *Exceptional Children,* Vol. 64, No. 1, PP 7-18, Council for Exceptional Children, 1997.

Heller, William and Kent Gerlach. Professional and ethical responsibilities of team members. In *Supervising Paraeducators in Educational Settings: A Team Approach,* edited by A.L. Pickett & K. Gerlach. Austin, TX: Pro-Ed, Inc., 2nd Edition, 2003.

Hilton, A. & K. Gerlach. Employment, Preparation and Management of Paraeducators: Challenges to Appropriate Service for Students With Disabilities, *Education and Training in Mental Retardation and Developmental Disabilities,* pp. 71-76, 1997.

IDEA Partnerships. *IDEA Partnerships Paraprofessional Initiative: Report to the U.S. Department of Education, Office of Special Education Programs.* Arlington, VA: Council for Exceptional Children, 2001.

Iowa Department of Education. *Guide for Effective Para-educator Practices in Iowa.* Des Moines, IA: 2008.

Lasater, Mary. *RTI and the Paraeducator's Roles: Effective Teaming.* Port Chester, NY: National Professional Resources, Inc., 2009.

Minnesota Paraprofessional Project, Institute on Community Integration, University of Minnesota. *Minnesota Paraprofessional Guide.* Minneapolis, MN, 2003.

No Child Left Behind Act of 2001, P.L. 107-110, 107th congress. Retrieved April 17, 2002, from www.ed.gov/legislation/ESEA02/, 2001.

Pickett, Anna Lou, and Kent Gerlach, eds. *Supervising Paraeducators in Educational Settings: A Team Approach.* Austin, TX: Pro-Ed, Inc., 2nd Edition, 2003.

Pickett, Anna L. *Strengthening and Supporting Teacher/Provider-Paraeducator Teams: Guidelines for Paraeducator's Roles, Supervision, and Preparation.* National Resource Center for Paraeducators in Special Education and Related Services, Center for Advanced Study in Education, the Graduate School and University Center, City University of New York, NY, 2000.

Shepard, Linda. *Classroom Aides Helper.* Palo Alto, CA: Volk Publishing, 1979.

Utah State Department Office of Special Education. *Utah State Standards for Paraeducators in Special Education.* Salt Lake City, Utah, 1995.

Web Sites

American Federation of Teachers (AFT): Standards for a Profession was founded in 1916 to represent the economical and professional interests of classroom teachers, AFT is an affiliated international union of teachers. www.aft.org.

B.E.S.T. Education Search by Topic enables search by key word or by the topic list or browsing of the Awards for extensive reviews of education sites. www.educationworld.com.

Center on Personnel Studies in Special Education (COPSSE) provides research focused on the preparation of special education professionals and its impact on beginning teacher quality and student outcomes. This research is intended to inform policymakers about advantages and disadvantages of preparation alternatives and the use of public funds in addressing personnel shortages. www.coe.ufl.edu/copsse/index.php.

Council for Exceptional Children offers information on CEC's knowledge and skill standards for beginning paraeducators in special education. www.cec.sped.org.

Council of Great City Schools contains links and resources, selected by this coalition, of school districts in the largest U.S. cities. www.cgcs.org.

The Education Trust is an independent non-profit organization whose mission is to make schools work for all of the young people they serve. The organization provides credible information on what works in high-performing, high-poverty schools. www.edtrust.org.

ERIC Database issues publications pertaining to paraprofessionals, US Department of Education. http://eric.ed.gov.

IMPACT explores the growing role of paraeducators in our schools. www.ici.umn.edu/products/impact.

The Minnesota Paraprofessional Consortium.
http://ici2.umn.edu/para.

National Clearinghouse for Paraeducators.
www.usc.edu/dept/education/CMMR/Clearinghouse.html.

National Coalition for Parent Involvement in Education (NCPIE) is a coalition of major education, community, public service and advocacy groups organized to create meaningful family-school partnerships in every school in America. Offers up-to-date information about policies and practices that impact education, and ways in which parents can become effective partners with schools in improving their children's education. www.ncpie.org.

The National Early Childhood Technical Assistance Center. www.ectac.org/topics/personnel/paraprof.asp.

National Education Association *provides educational support for professionals.* www.nea.org.

National Joint Committee on Learning Disabilities focuses on ethical responsibilities, educational requirements, roles and responsibilities of paraprofessionals, plus responsibilities of qualified teacher/service providers for those with learning disabilities. www.ldonline.org.

National Resource Center for Paraprofessionals addresses policy questions and other needs of the field, providing technical assistance and sharing information about management practices, regulatory procedures, and training that enables administrators and staff developers to improve the recruitment, depth of supervision and career development of paraprofessionals. www.nrcpara.org. A page for all 50 states' programs. http://nrcpara.org/states.

PARA2 Center University of Colorado in Denver.
www.paracenter.org.

Paraeducator Support of Students with Disabilities in General Education Classrooms, University of Vermont. www.uvm.edu/~cdci/parasupport/.

Paraprofessional Database Research Navigator, compiled by the Education Commission of the States, has a large amount of research from the 50 states regarding paraprofessional certification and qualifications requirements, development for paraprofessionals and assessment tests and passing scores for those who are accepted. www.ecs.org.

Project Para—University of Nebraska Lincoln Online Training. www.para.unl.edu.

Resource Site for Paraeducator Supervision. http://ici.umn.edu/para/teachers.

Rhode Island Teacher Assistants Project focuses on policy, skill standards and training for teacher assistants. www.ritap.org/ritap.

Special Education News focuses on special education and current legislation effecting paraeducators. www.special ednews.com.

Study of Personnel Needs in Special Education (SPeNSE) was designed to address concerns about nation-wide shortages in the number of personnel for students with disabilities and the need for improvement in the qualifications of those employees. Part of a national assessment of the Individuals with Disabilities Act mandated by Congress, SPeNSE examined the extent to which personnel are adequately prepared to work with students with disabilities, variation in personnel preparation and factors that affect that variation. http://ferdig.coe.ufl.edu/spense.

Technology, Research, and Innovation in Special Education provides information on training programs for paraprofessionals and supervising teachers. Includes links to dozens of other sites. www.trisped.org.

U.S. Department of Education. www.ed.gov.

Utah State Paraeducator Website lists Utah standards, knowledge and skills competencies for paraeducators and professional development. http://utahpara.org.

Washington State Paraeducator. www.k12.wa.us/Paraeducators/.

Working with Paraeducators, University of Kansas has a section with information, worksheets, case studies, etc., for teachers who supervise paraeducators. http://specialconnections.ku.edu.

Glossary of Terms

Accommodations: Teaching supports and services that the student may require to successfully demonstrate learning. Accommodations should not change expectations to the curriculum grade levels. Examples include, extra time for assignments or tests, the use of taped textbooks, use of a study carrel, etc.

Accountability: Measurable proof that teachers, schools, districts and states are teaching students efficiently and well, usually measured in the form of student success rates on various tests.

Achievement Gap: Persistent differences in achievement among different groups of students as indicated by scores on standardized tests, teacher grades and other data. The gaps most frequently referred to are those between whites and minority groups, especially African-Americans and Hispanics.

Achievement Test: A test used to measure how a student has learned in various school subjects/curriculum.

Adequate Yearly Progress (AYP): An individual state's measure of yearly progress toward achieving academic standards. "Adequate Yearly Progress" is the minimum level improvement that states, school districts and schools must achieve each year. The report is done annually.

Advocate: An individual who represents or speaks out on behalf of another person's interests (as in a parent or guardian with his/her child).

Alignment: The effort to ensure that what teachers teach is matched to what the curriculum says will be taught and what will be assessed.

Alternate Assessment: Use of assessment strategies, such as performance assessment and portfolios, to replace or supplement assessment by machine-scored, multiple-choice tests.

Alternative Dispute Resolution: A spectrum of dispute resolution processes, ranging from informal discussion to formal decision (such as, Mediation, IEP Facilitation, Ombudsperson) identified under the federal law, IDEA.

Americans with Disabilities Act (ADA): A federal law enacted in 1992 which defines "disability" and prohibits discrimination by employers, by any facility open to the general public, and/or by state and local public agencies that provide such services as transportation (Public Law 101-336).

Applied Behavior Analysis (ABA): An intensive, structured teaching program where behaviors to be taught are broken down into their simplest elements. These elements are taught using repeated trials where the student is presented with a stimulus. Correct responses and behaviors are rewarded with positive reinforcement. When incorrect responses occur, they are ignored and appropriate responses are prompted and rewarded.

Appropriate: The ability to meet a need that is suitable or fitting the student's individual needs and abilities.

Assessment: Measurement of the learning and performance of students or teachers. Different types of formal or informal assessment instruments include achievement tests, minimum competency tests, developmental screening tests, aptitude tests, observation instruments, performance tasks and authentic assessments.

Assistive Technology: Any item, piece of equipment, technology or product system (whether acquired commercially or off the shelf) modified or customized, that is used to increase, maintain or improve functional capabilities of individuals with disabilities.

Behavior Intervention Plan (BIP): A plan that is put in place to teach a student proper behavior and social skills. The plan should be positive in nature, not punitive.

Benchmarks/Standards: A standard for judging a performance. Some schools develop benchmarks to tell what students should know by a particular stage of their schooling; for example, "by the end of sixth grade, students should be able to locate major cities and other geographical features on each of the continents."

Bilingualism: The ability to read, speak, understand, and write well in two or more languages

Bilingual Education: An in-school program for students whose first language is not English or who have limited English skills. Bilingual education provides English language development plus subject area instruction in the student's native language. The goal is for the student to gain knowledge and be literate in two languages.

Charter School: A self-governing educational facility that operates under a contract between the school's organizers and the sponsors (often local school boards, but sometimes other agencies, such as state boards of education). The organizers are often teachers, parents, or private organizations. The charter may detail the school's instructional design, methods of assessment, management and finances.

Child Study Team: A group of school staff that may include teachers, therapists, psychologists or social workers who meet for the purpose of making programming decisions concerning students who are struggling in school or who are suspected of having a disability.

Cognitive Learning: The mental processes involved in learning, such as remembering and understanding facts and ideas.

Common Core State Standards (CCSS): Developed by the Council of Chief State School Officers, the Common Core State Standards are a set of high-quality academic standards in English language arts and mathematics. The CCSS have been adopted by many state education departments throughout the U.S.

Communication Skills: The ability to provide and receive information in an effective manner.

Competencies: The specific skills and knowledge required for employment in various programs and position levels.

Complaint: A written notice by a parent or other interested party sent to the department of special education claiming that the local school district has violated a requirement of federal or state law concerning special education program of a specific child.

Coordinating and Planning Skills: The ability to see that roles and responsibilities are scheduled appropriately, resources are available when needed, and conferences and meetings are used to their fullest advantage.

Curriculum: A written plan outlining what students will be taught (a course of study). For example, the curriculum of an elementary school usually includes language arts, mathematics, science, social studies and other subjects.

Cumulative File: The general file of a student's records maintained by the school. A parent has the right to inspect the file and have copies of any information contained in it.

Delegating Skills: The ability to communicate responsibilities effectively to another member of the team.

Due Process: The actions that protect an individual's rights. In special education, this applies to those actions taken to protect the educational rights of students with disabilities.

Early Intervention Services: A provision under IDEA. It allows school districts to use IDEA Part B funds to provide services and support for students in grades K-12 who have not been identified as needing special education or related services, but who need additional academic and behavioral support to succeed in a general education environment.

Elementary and Secondary Education Act (ESEA): Originally enacted in 1965, this act provides federal funding for elementary and secondary education including Title I funding for students from low-income families.. The most recent reauthorization in 2001 is called the No Child Left Behind Act (NCLB).

Eligibility: To be eligible for special education under IDEA, a student must have a disability and must need special education services and/or related services. IDEA lists 13 separate categories of eligibility. To determine if a student is eligible under one of the areas of exceptionality, an individualized evaluation of the student must be conducted.

English Language Learner (ELL): A student whose first language is other than English and who is in a special program for learning English (which may be bilingual education or English as a second language program).

Evaluation: A process using observation, testing and test analysis to determine a student's strengths and weaknesses in order to plan his/her educational program.

Extended School Year (ESY): Special education and related services provided to a student in accordance with a student's IEP beyond the normal school year (for example, summer school) and is provided at no cost to parents. The determination of the need for ESY services to a student is determined by the IEP team or PPT on an individual basis.

Family Educational Rights and Privacy Act (FERPA): A federal law enacted in 1984 that provides all parents of students (as well as students over the age of 18 or attending post-secondary schools) the right to review, correct and control access to their student's records.

Feedback Skills: The ability of the supervisor to monitor performance of the paraeducator through appropriate observation and feedback to ensure team effectiveness.

Focused Monitoring: A compliance and technical assistance model designed to be both a performance measurement and a compliance tool to ensure that states are effectively implementing requirements of the IDEA. Focused monitoring involves the selection of a limited number of priority performance areas accompanied by a limited number of indicators, benchmarks and triggers.

Free, Appropriate Public Education (FAPE): One of the key requirements of IDEA, which requires that an education program be provided for all school-aged children (regardless of disability) without cost to families; the exact requirements of "appropriate" are not defined, but other references within the law imply the most appropriate setting available.

Functional Behavior Assessment (FBA): An assessment that looks at why a student behaves the way he/she does, given the nature of the student and what is happening in the environment. It is a process for collecting data to determine the possible causes of problem behaviors and to identify strategies to address those behaviors.

Goal: A result to be achieved

Guiding Principals: A statement of beliefs that provide a philosophical framework that state and local educational agencies can build upon to ensure appropriate team roles, supervision, professional development and respect for para-educators.

High-Stakes Testing: Tests used to determine which individual students receive rewards, honors, or sanctions. Examples of tests with high stakes attached include college entrance examinations and tests which students must pass to be promoted to the next grade or to graduate from high school.

Inclusion: The practice of placing students with disabilities in general education classrooms environments with their non-disabled peers. Also sometimes referred to as "main-streaming."

Independent Evaluation: An evaluation performed by a certified and/or licensed professional examiner who is not employed by the school system responsible for the education of the student.

Individualized Education Program (IEP): A written education program for a student with a disability that is developed by a team of professionals (administrators, teachers, therapists, etc.) and the student's parents. The IEP is reviewed and updated yearly and describes the student's present level of performance, what the student's learning needs are, what services the student will need (when and for how long) and identifies who will provide the services.

IEP Team: A group of professionals who represent a multi-disciplinary team of teaching, administrative and pupil personnel staff and who, with the parents, are equal participants in the decision-making process to determine the specific educational needs of the student. The IEP team develops, reviews and revises a student's Individualized Education Plan (IEP). Sometimes this team is also referred to as a Planning and Placement Team (PPT).

Individuals with Disabilities Education Act (IDEA): The federal law governing special education originally passed in 1975, requiring that public schools provide a "free, appropriate public education" to children ages 3-21, regardless of the disability. IDEA was reauthorized in 2004 and is titled Individuals with Disabilities Education Improvement Act (IDEIA) (2004).

Interpersonal Skills: The ability to recognize and demonstrate appropriate social behaviors, work with different interpersonal styles and appreciate the uniqueness of others, and manage conflict.

Least Restrictive Environment (LRE): An educational setting that provides a student with disabilities the chance to work and learn to the best of his or her ability. LRE also provides a student with as much contact as possible with peers without disabilities, while meeting the student's learning needs and physical requirements.

Local Education Agency (LEA): Public schools operating as independent districts in accordance with statues, regulations and policies of the each state's education agency or Department of Education.

Manifestation Determination: When a student with a disability engages in inappropriate behavior or breaks a rule or code of conduct that applies to non-disabled students and the school proposes to remove the student, the school must hold a hearing to determine if the student's inappropriate behavior was caused by the disability.

Mediation: A voluntary process that allows parties to resolve their dispute without litigation, it cannot be used to deny or delay parents' rights to a due process hearing. A qualified and impartial mediator helps parents and schools express their views and positions in order to reach a mutual agreement.

Mission: A statement of what the school district or team is about and the unique contribution it can make

Modifications: Changes made to the curriculum expectations in order to meet the needs of the student. Modifications are made when the expectations are beyond the student's level of ability. Modifications may be minimal or very complex depending on the student's performance and must be clearly acknowledged in the student's IEP.

Monitoring: Activities designed to ensure that specific regulations or procedures are being carried out. For example, parents may monitor the IEP written for their child; or state education agencies are required to establish monitoring procedures to determine the degree to which local education agencies are meeting the requirements of IDEA at the local level.

No Child Left Behind Act (NCLB): The 2001 reauthorization of the federal Elementary and Secondary Education Act. NCLB supports standards-based education reform.

Objective: A specific point of measurement that the team intends to meet in pursuit of its goals.

Occupational Therapy: A therapy or treatment that helps individual development of physical skills that will aid in daily living. It focuses on sensory integration, coordination of movement, fine motor and self-help skills, such as dressing, feeding, etc.

Office of Civil Rights (OCR): A branch of the U.S. Department of Education that enforces several federal civil rights laws (such as Section 504) that prohibit discrimination in programs or activities that receive federal financial assistance. These laws prohibit discrimination on the basis of race, national origin, sex, disability and on the basis of age.

Office of Special Education Programs (OSEP): A division of the U.S. Department of Education dedicated to improving results for children with disabilities, ages birth through 21, by providing leadership and financial support to assist states and local districts. OSEP administers the Individuals with Disabilities Education Act (IDEA).

Paraeducator: A school employee who assists and supports teacher-directed instruction. Other titles used to identify these employees may include: paraprofessional, teacher aide/assistant, education technician, transition trainer, job coach, therapy assistant, home visitor and many others.

Paraeducator Management and Supervision: Responsibility for the management and supervision of paraeducators is divided into two components:

> ▶ Administrative Personnel have operational responsibility for establishing and carrying out personnel practices connected with paraeducator employment, preparation, evaluation and dismissal.

> ▶ Teachers/Providers have responsibility for supervising and integrating paraeducators into learning

environments, including planning, scheduling, monitoring and providing feedback to paraeducators.

Parental Involvement: The participation of parents in regular two-way, meaningful communication involving student academic learning and behavior, as well as other school activities. The involvement includes ensuring that parents play an integral role in assisting their child's learning, that parents are encouraged to be actively involved as full partners in their child's education at school, and are included, as appropriate, in decision making and on advisory committees to assist in their child's education.

Performance Standards: What a student is supposed to be able to do by the end of a particular grade.

Physical Therapy: A therapy option for physical disabilities that includes the use of massage, exercise, etc. to help the individual improve the use of bones, muscles, joints and nerves utilized in gross motor activities.

Plan: A time-phased action sequence used to guide and coordinate activities in pursuit of objectives.

Present Level of Educational Performance: Statements written in the IEP that accurately describe the student's strengths, weaknesses and learning styles.

Prior Written Notice: A procedural safeguard that says school districts must inform parents of their rights. Specifically, the school must inform parents of any actions proposed or refused by the IEP or PPT team, any alternatives that were discussed, as well as the assessment information used to make the decision—and they must do so in writing.

Problem-Solving Skills: The ability to identify issues and propose, evaluate, and analyze alternative solutions in order to develop ways of implementing a plan for the problem.

Proficiency: Refers to an ability or skill of a high degree. Sometimes referred to as "mastery."

Program Implementation Teams: Smaller teams that have day-to-day responsibility for providing education and other direct services to students and their families. Program implementation teams are found in inclusive general education classrooms, special education classrooms, Title I programs, multilingual/ESL programs, early childhood and school-to-work/vocational programs.

Program Planning Team (PPT): Also referred to as an IEP team, a Program Planning Team (PPT) is a multi-disciplinary team of school professionals responsible for developing an Individualized Education Plan (IEP). Team members often include general and special education teachers, related services personnel, parents and others involved in the student's education.

Related Services: Transportation, developmental, corrective and other supportive services that a student with disabilities requires in order to benefit from special education. They also include speech pathology and audiology, psychological services, physical and occupational therapy, recreation, counseling services and medical services for diagnostic and evaluation purposes, school health services, social work services in school and parent counseling/training.

Response to Intervention (RTI): RTI is a regular education model that refers to a tiered approach to instruction. This model is used to promote the early identification of students who may be at risk for learning or behavioral difficulties and provide them as soon as possible with additional supports, beginning in the general education classroom.

School Reform: The implementation of new organizational patterns or styles of leadership and management to bring about renewed, more effective schools. Examples may include reorganizing the school day or allocating more decision-making power to teachers and/or involving parents in decision making.

School Social Worker: Professionals who provide a vital communication link between school personnel and the family of the student with a disability. They are frequently involved in parent contact, parent interviews and contact with support service personnel within the community, as well as individual pupil evaluation and school-home pupil programming and follow-up.

Section 504 of the Rehabilitation Act of 1973: A Civil Rights Act that ensures that no individual with a disability can be excluded from a free, appropriate public education and employment.

Sensory Integration Disorder (SID or SI): Also known as Sensory Integration Dysfunction—the ability to process information received through the senses, causing problems with learning, development and behavior.

Special Education: Specially designed instruction to meet the unique needs of students with disabilities.

Speech/Language Therapy: A planned program to improve and correct speech and/or language or communication problems.

Standards: In current usage, the term usually refers to specific criteria for what students are expected to learn and be able to do. These standards usually take two forms in the curriculum:

> ▶ Content Standards: Tell what students are expected to know and be able to do in various subject areas, such as mathematics and science.

▸ Performance Standards: Specify what levels of learning are expected. Performance standards assess the degree to which content standards have been met. In recent years, standards have also been developed specifying what teachers should know and be able to do.

State Education Agency (SEA): The agency primarily responsible for the supervision of a given state's public elementary and secondary schools. Often referred to as the state's Department of Education.

Strategy: A set of rules and guidelines to assist orderly progression toward a teams goals and objectives

Supplementary Aids and Services: Aids, services, program modifications, and/or supports for school personnel that are provided in regular education classes or other education-related settings to enable students with disabilities to be educated with students who are non-disabled.

Supplemental Educational Services (SES): Under the federal No Child Left Behind Act, students from low-income families who are attending schools that have been identified as in need of improvement for two years will be eligible to receive outside tutoring or academic assistance. Parents can choose the appropriate services for their child from a list of approved providers. The school district will purchase the services.

Tactile Defensiveness: An abnormal sensitivity to touch, indicated by avoidance or rejection of touching and handling. The student may resist touching or being touched by something that is wet, of an unusual texture or unfamiliar temperature or pressure.

Teamwork Skills: The ability of the supervisor to interface with the paraeducator in a manner that promotes teamwork and develops commitment.

Technical and Management Skills: The ability to understand the mission of the team and program. The supervising professional must schedule, plan, and manage time and handle the unexpected.

Title I: Provision of federal funding to schools to help students who are behind academically or at risk of falling behind. Funding is based on the number of low-income students in the school, generally those eligible for the free lunch program. Title I is intended to supplement, not to replace state and district funds.

Transition: The movement from one service, location or program to another. Young students with disabilities transition at age three from early intervention to preschool special education services or to other community settings and services. Adolescents transition from school to adult services.

Universal Design for Learning (UDL): The design of products and environments to be useable by all individuals, to the greatest extent possible, without the need for adaptation or specialized design. Its purpose is to increase students' access to the general curriculum by reducing physical, cognitive, intellectual and other barriers to learning.

Vocational Education: Formal training designed to prepare individuals to work in a certain job or occupational area, such as construction, cosmetology, food service or electronics.

Abbreviations/Acronyms

ABA	Applied Behavior Analysis
ADA	Americans with Disabilities Act
ADD	Attention Deficit Disorder
ADHD	Attention Deficit Hyperactivity Disorder
AE	Age Equivalent
AFT	American Federation of Teachers
ASHA	American Speech and Hearing Association
AT	Assistive Technology
BD	Behavior Disorders
BOE	Board of Education
CA	Chronological Age
CCLS	Common Core Learning Standards
CCSS	Common Core State Standards
CD	Communication Disorder
CEC	Council for Exceptional Children
CF	Cumulative File
CPS	Child Protective Services
DD	Developmental Disabilities
DOB	Date of Birth
DOH	Department of Health
DSHS	Department of Social and Health Services
DVR	Division of Vocational Rehabilitation
EA	Educational Assistant
EBD	Emotional/Behavioral Disorder
ECE	Early Childhood Education
ECEAP	Early Childhood Education and Assistance Program
EI	Early Intervention
ELL	English Language Learner
ESEA	Elementary/Secondary Educational Act
ESL	English as a Second Language

ESY	Extended School Year
FAPE	Free Appropriate Public Education
FERPA	Family Educational Right to Privacy Act
FAS	Fetal Alcohol Syndrome
FBA	Functional Behavior Assessment
FTE	Full Time Equivalency
FOC	Focus of Concern
GE	Grade Equivalent
GPA	Grade Point Average
HHS	Department of Health and Human Services (US)
HI	Hearing Impaired
HR	Human Resources
HUD	Department of Housing and Urban Development (US)
IA	Instructional Assistant
IDEA	Individuals with Disabilities Education Act
IE	Independent evaluation
IEP	Individualized Education Program
IHP	Individualized Health Plan
IFSP	Individualized Family Service Plan
IQ	Intelligence Quotient
ITEIP	Infant Toddler Early Intervention Program
LAP	Learning Assistance Program
LAS	Language Assessment Scales (assessing second language students)
LD	Learning Disability
LEA	Local Educational Agency
LPN	Licensed Practical Nurse
LRE	Least Restrictive Environment
MA	Mental Age
MD	Multiple Disabilities
MH	Mental Health
NCLB	No Child Left Behind

NEA	National Educational Association
OCR	Office for Civil Rights
OSEP	Office of Special Education Programs
OSPI	Office of the Superintendent of Public Instruction
OT	Occupational Therapist/Therapy
PE	Physical Education
PLEP	Present Levels of Educational Performance
PPT	Program Planning Team
PR	Percentile Rank
PS	Performance Standards
PT	Physical Therapist/Therapy
PTA	Parent Teacher Association
RN	Registered Nurse
RS	Related Services
S504	Section 504 of the Rehabilitation Act of 1973
SDI	Specifically Designed Instruction
SE	Special Education (more commonly Sp. Ed., when abbreviated)
SEA	State educational Agency
SES	Supplemental Educational Services
SLP	Speech-Language Pathologist
SSI	Supplemental Security Income
SST	School Support Team
ST	Speech Therapy
SY	School year
TA	Teaching Assistant
TAP	Targeted Assistance Program
TBI	Traumatic Brain Injury
UDL	Universal Design for Learning
VE	Vocational Education
VI	Visually Impaired

What Motivates Members of the Team

✓ Working in challenging roles

✓ Being treated fairly

✓ Being appreciated

✓ Knowing what they do is of value

✓ Feeling important

✓ Feeling needed

✓ Doing a good job and being recognized for it

✓ Being able to make a difference

We can create a positive atmosphere in which team members feel their needs are being met by

✓ Sharing ideas and information

✓ Providing training and development

✓ Being available when needed

✓ Providing resources, assistance, and support

✓ Demonstrating and observing

✓ Seeking feedback input and ideas

✓ Listening

✓ Working to solve problems together

—Adapted from an unknown source